Pro Wrestling Kids' Style

BY

Shawn "Crusher" Crossen

PRO WRESTLING KIDS' STYLE

THE MOST AMAZING UNTOLD STORY IN PROFESSIONAL WRESTLING HISTORY

BY

Shawn "Crusher" Crossen

NWF BOOKS

NWF Books
5104 Chadwick Street
Schofield, WI 54476

Homepage: http://www.nwfwrestling.net
Email: crusherc@aol.com
Telephone: 715-355-0895

ISBN: 1-879000-12-1 (Cloth)

The text was set in 12 point Myriad Pro by J.H. Banner.
Printed in the United States of America by Thomson-Shore.

Second Edition

The paper used in this publication meets the minimum requirements of the American National Standard for Information Sciences Permanence of Paper for Printed Library Materials Z39.48-1992 (R1997).

This book is dedicated to all former participants of *NWF Kids Pro Wrestling* during the years of 1984 through 1988.

For without your loyal support and dedication to our league, all that we accomplished would have never been possible.

Table of Contents

Chapter 1
The Beginning

It's amazing to look back at it today and see just how much we actually accomplished. To look back at how we started out and see just how successful we became within just a few short years, it really is quite amazing. Of course these days, small-time wrestling leagues that involve kids are basically a dime a dozen, and they refer to them as *backyard wrestling* leagues. But in 1984, rest assured, we were the only ones doing it. The phrase *backyard wrestling* did not exist then, and we never considered ourselves as such. As far as we were concerned, we were just another league—like the American Wrestling Association or the National Wrestling Alliance—only we were comprised of kids. But back in 1984 when I was at the age of 14, if you would have told me that in less than two years, I would be promoting live *house shows* in front of hundreds of paid spectators throughout the metro area with our wrestling show, which in addition to that, would be airing all across the country, I would have never believed you. But by 1986, we had a weekly show airing on cable TV nationwide. We had announcers, good guys, bad guys, title belts, and a full-sized professional wrestling ring … but wait, I'm getting ahead of myself. I guess we need to start from the beginning.

One of my best friends growing up was Charley Lane. He was a few years younger than me, but that never bothered us. We were both roughly the same size and build, and while growing up, we did everything together. The birth of our wrestling league stemmed back to one very important phone call that would eventually change everything up to that point in my life. It's amazing to think that had I not made this phone call, then our kids pro wrestling league just may have never even happened. It's at times like this where one simple action you do ends up dictating the course of history that you take.

Shawn Crossen at age 14 from 1984.

It was 1981, and I was eleven years old at the time. I remember it well: It was a Sunday morning, and I picked up the phone and called Charley to see what he was doing. He answered the phone with a "Hello," and I could tell by his tone that he was feeling impatient. I said, "Hey, what's going on?" Charley quickly replied, "I gotta go … I'll call you back!" Not knowing why he was being so hesitant to talk, I said, "Wait, Charley. What's going on?" And after a few more times back and forth, Charley finally shouted out, "Hulk Hogan's got a pair of brass knuckles, and he is going to hit Nick Bockwinkle. I'll call you back!" And with that, he slammed the receiver down. I knew Charley was watching wrestling, so I figured I would turn it on and see just what he was getting so excited about.

I turned to Channel 9, and I started to watch this match unfold between Hogan and Bockwinkle from the St. Paul Civic Center. This was the same match Charley was watching. And as I watched it, I saw Hogan take away the brass knuckles from Bockwinkle, use them against his opponent and win the AWA championship as the fans went completely wild. But in the interview to follow, announcer Mean Gene Okerlund quickly pointed out that the championship belt was being returned back to Bockwinkle, due to the use of the foreign object by Hogan. And so through watching all of this, I got hooked. What had Charley's undivided attention now had consumed me as well, and I became an instant *Hulkamaniac*. It was 1981, and even though Hulk Hogan had not yet made an instant impact nationwide as he did when he joined the WWF a few years later, *Hulkamania* was indeed running wild in the Midwest.

Charley Lane at age 12 from 1984.

For the next two years, I became obsessed with professional wrestling. Charley and I watched wrestling every Sunday morning, and Hogan was our biggest reason why. Each month, the AWA held matches at the St. Paul Civic Center, and we went to a few of the cards throughout the early 1980s. I remember being at the sold-out Civic Center on *Super Sunday* in front of 30,000-plus fans for yet another title match between Hulk Hogan and Nick Bockwinkle in May of 1983. I remember when Hogan made his entrance to Survivor's hit song, "Eye of the Tiger," the electricity of excitement became so thick, so intense, that you could cut it with a knife. This level of high energy was one of the main reasons I loved professional wrestling. And Hulk Hogan was a big part of that excitement. You have to understand that going into this match, everyone was talking about how Hulk Hogan was going to win the AWA title once and for all. I remember a week prior to this match seeing legendary AWA promoter Wally Karbo interrupt a Hogan interview and tell the Hulk that if he could just maintain his temper during the upcoming match, we'd have a new World Champion that night. And then Hogan got all excited—along with the rest of us watching at home. During the match, Hogan accidentally back-body-dropped Bockwinkle over the top rope, and later on, Hogan pinned Bockwinkle to win the title. But AWA president Stanley Blackburn, who was at ringside, eventually reversed the decision due to Hogan throwing Bockwinkle over the top rope, and the fans went nuts. We could not believe it. How could Hogan get robbed again? At the time, I hated it. But from a promoter's standpoint, it was brilliant. If you had 30,000 fans wanting to see Hogan win the title that night, just how many would come back for the rematch next month? Hogan went on to become famous worldwide in the WWF, but nothing would ever replace those earlier years while he was in the AWA. In those days, Hogan was pure, he was genuine, and he was like nothing the wrestling business had ever seen before.

It was sometime in January of 1984, when the salesman from Group W Cable came knocking at our door. You see, back in those days, if you were interested in getting cable TV, they would send sales people to your house to show you all the different packages that were available. During his sales presentation, he mentioned that Group W Cable offers the use of a public access program to all members of the community, where you can use video equipment at no charge and produce your own cable TV shows that are then aired on cable TV. I was extremely taken at the chance to do this. I remember I kept going back to this opportunity during his presentation by saying, "You mean to tell me, I can make my own TV shows?" It must have drove the salesman and my parents nuts, but just the thought of seeing yourself on television doing your own TV show, it was something I was extremely interested in doing.

I wanted to get started right away, so I wasted no time in going down to the Group W Cable offices and taking the classes to learn how to use the equipment. The first class was on the *port-a-pak* equipment. The class basically taught the ability to check out the remote cameras so that you can videotape your projects. Then, I also had to take a course on *editing*, which enabled me to edit the video together for an adequately produced TV show. So now that I had learned how to use the equipment, what kind of show was I going to produce? At first, I had no idea. I was in such a hurry to learn how to use all this stuff, yet I did not have a clue as to what I was going to produce with it. After trying several different "skit" type shows, nothing was really working. And then came the idea.

Chapter 2
The Kids Quad Cities
Pro Wrestling Show

Now to this day, it is not clear to who actually thought of the idea. But between Charley and myself, we somehow came up with the concept for a *kids pro wrestling* show. It was going to be a TV show like the professional versions; only it would involve kids— like a *little league* of professional wrestling. Growing up, it always bothered me that professional wrestling wasn't represented in little league sports, so what better reason than that alone to start this league of ours? As we started the league, all of us involved referred to it as *The Wrestling Show*, because that was basically what it was. Besides Charley and myself, the initial cast of wrestlers included Milton Warner, Mark Ackermann, Todd Kampa, Chris Daniels, and Matt Denny. We were all about the same age, averaging 13 years old. So now that we had the concept, the next thing to figure out was where to have our matches. At first, Milton had mentioned that there was an actual ring in the basement of Fred Moore Jr. High School used by the local chapter of Golden Gloves Boxing, and he thought that would work well. This would have been perfect, so Milton and myself met with the community school director at Fred Moore, Mr. Daniels, and we told him about our plans and asked for permission to use the ring. He looked at us like we were crazy and simply replied, "I don't think this would be a good idea at all." And that was that.

We were all bummed out about not getting to use the ring, but as they say, the show must go on. So at that point, we decided to turn my basement into a makeshift wrestling ring/studio by using some old bed mattresses. It certainly was not as good as an actual ring would have been, but it would work for now. We figured that we could all save our money and then build ourselves a ring someday, and that would be a good goal to work towards. Besides, the fun part of doing the actual wrestling itself did not require a ring anyway. So even though we didn't have a ring, we made up for it by creating entertaining rivalries between our characters, as they wrestled in the ring and quarreled during heated pre-match and post-match interviews. As one could expect, our main objective was making the show appear *real* to viewers watching at home. In order to sell the hits, body slams, and falls to those watching, we had to create black eyes, blood, and bruises. To accomplish this end, I would normally take items from my sister's makeup collection in preparation for our videotaping. And then after our matches ended, we would do ourselves up with intense-looking-but-fake bruises and black eyes. Getting fake blood during any part of the year outside of Halloween season, on the other hand, was impossible. So I would make fake blood using liquid soap and red food coloring. Then, we would put the "blood" in small plastic bags that were hidden around the ring area (mattresses). And when a match called for blood, you would take one of these bags and pop it open on the head of your opponent (all of this action hidden from camera view, of course). And just like that, the blood would appear. It really worked quite well.

Charley "Luxury" Lane with a black eye and bruises.

On camera, the characters we had in the first few shows were quite interesting. There was myself, Shawn Crossen, known as *Crusher Crossen* in the ring. As for the name, well, *Crusher* just went well with Crossen, and if the shoe fits, then wear it, I guess. As for my style, I was trying to be a Hulk Hogan type, and although I acted the part well, I did not look it at all. Charley Lane was *Luxury Lane*— once again, a name combination that went well together. His style was very similar to that of Jesse The Body Ventura, and his dad even looked like Jesse The Body. Chris Daniels was *Tuffer Daniels*, in which he used the nickname *Tuffer* that he went by at home and around our neighborhood. Todd Kampa wrestled as *Todd the Killer Kampa* and always reminded me of Mr. Wonderful Paul Orndorf. Milton Warner and Mark Ackermann formed a tag team and wrestled in masks calling themselves *The Destruction Masters* and would be similar to that of The Super Destroyers from late 1970s fame. As for Matt Denny, he just went by Matt Denny. Matt was a chubby kid, much overweight, so his style would be compared to Jerry Blackwell or King Kong Bundy. And that made up our initial cast of wrestlers in the beginning.

Chris "the Tuffer" Daniels from early 1984.

I remember after we taped and edited our first show. It was set to premiere on cable TV a week or so later, and I invited all the guys over to watch it. The first show was simply titled *The Kids Quad Cities Pro Wrestling Show*. I remember how excited we all were as we watched ourselves on TV for the first time that night. Just seeing ourselves on the TV and knowing that we were being watched all over town was pretty incredible to us. At the time, our show was seen in only four Minnesota towns: Anoka, Champlin, Ramsey, and Andover. But it could have been the entire country as far as we were concerned. This was back when there were only 35 to 40 cable channels at the most, so the odds of people channel surfing and landing on our wrestling show were pretty good.

After the first few shows, the buzz was out in school regarding our wrestling show. I can remember many kids noticing me in school. They either asked questions about the show or made fun of it. The latter never bothered me, as I enjoyed the show too much. Whenever people made fun of it, I would just say, "It's so fun doing it, I could care less what you think," and they were always left speechless after that. In the beginning, it really was fun. And I mean *fun*. I mean, how could it not be? If we were not having fun, then what would be the purpose of doing it in the first place? Having fun with it was rule number one. And we were all having a blast with the show at the time.

Charley Lane interviewing champion
Shawn Crossen from early 1984.

On the third show, two new kids joined the roster. The first was Mike Ackermann, the younger brother of Mark. Where Mark was my age, Mike was a couple years younger and the same age as Charley. Mike did not have a wrestling name at first, but later on he would call himself *Merciful Mike Ackermann*. After a few shows, Mark pointed out to his brother that his name actually meant "full of mercy," so with that, Mike quickly changed his name to *Merciless Mike Ackermann*. His character was a lot like a Brad Reighganns or a Bob Backlund, somewhat stocky with a determined-to-win attitude. The other new guy was Robby Jacob, who was brought in for a different reason. Up to this point, we did not have a regular announcer or match commentator on our show. Prior to joining, Rob told me that being a sports announcer was something he had always wanted to do. So it was perfect that he become our league's master of ceremonies, the voice of *The Kids Quad Cities Pro Wrestling Show*.

Rob Jacob joins as the league's first announcer in 1984.

After taping a few more shows in my basement, Charley and I decided to take Group W Cable's *studio production course*, which would allow us to use the company's actual production studio. This studio featured multiple video cameras, professional style ¾-inch tape decks, and a control room complete with an audio mixing board and character generator. But best of all, they had a wooden stage in the studio that we could use as our new ring. Granted it did not have the four posts or ropes to make it a true ring, it was a lot better than those old mattresses down in my basement. So once Charley and I completed the course, we booked some studio time and taped our first show in the Group W Cable Studio. Although it was the same show we were doing in the basement, it seemed to take on a new and more professional look. The show actually started to resemble professional wrestling that you'd see on TV.

*New stage in studio serves as the NWF's new home
in the summer of 1984.*

Up to this point in time, I was the Quad Cities World Champion. Charley wanted to be the champion, but being older, I talked him out of it and said he could be the tag team champion with Kampa as his partner instead, and he went for that idea. But after Show #4 when he and Kampa lost the titles to The Destruction Masters, once again Charley was bugging me to lose my belt to him. But because I loved being champion so much, I managed to talk Charley out of it by making up a new title just for him. We invented the *PWA (Pacific Wrestling Association)* championship, and Charley became its titleholder. It was sort of an intercontinental title belt. In the beginning, the belts were made out of cardboard and tinfoil—not the best-looking things, but they passed as title belts, I guess. In time, though, we would have very attractive-looking belts. Moving forward, at Show #7, our second taping in Group W Cable studios, after much pressure from all the guys in the show, I decided to lose the Quad Cities belt for the first time. Mike Ackermann and myself were in the middle of a pretty big rivalry, so it seemed only fitting to drop the title to him. But it was an emotional thing for me, because deep down I did not want to lose that belt. Up to this point, my character had always been a heel of sorts, and Mike was definitely a baby face. At the end of the match in which I relinquished the belt to Mike, I raised his hand in victory in order to symbolically pass the torch, if you will, similar in gesture to the way Hogan did years later to his rival, The Ultimate Warrior. After that match, Mike and I went on to become great friends both in and out of the ring and formed a tag team on the show as well, and the *Crusher/Merciless Family* was born. But something was about to happen that nearly ended the wrestling show for good.

Chapter 3
The Studio Days

    In the summer of 1984, Charley and I got into a fight. We grew up as best friends, so getting into fights now and then was only natural. But this one was pretty bad. It concerned me hanging around some new kids I met down the street, and Charley was jealous. So we got into an argument one day, and he said our friendship was over. And for weeks, we did not talk to one another. And all this time, there was no wrestling show being done. You have to understand that, in the beginning, the wrestling show only existed because of Charley and myself. So, without one or the other, there was no show. The fact was that in order for the show to continue, it required both of us, and that's just the way it was. About a month went by when one day I was down at the local Holiday Gas Station on Main Street to get a slush puppy, and I ran into Milton Warner. Milton asked me why we had not taped a wrestling show in such a long time. I told him we hadn't made a show recently because Charley and I were fighting. And I remember Milton shaking his head and saying, "Man, you guys are stupid. You had a pretty good thing going with that show. I think you should talk to Charley and make up and start doing it again, because you guys had something good going with the wrestling show." It has been nearly 20 years since that time, but I can still remember those exact words from Milton. So I did what Milton said, and by the following week, we were back in the studio taping Show #8.

    A few new faces joined our roster while a few others quit the show. Jeff Ortel, the cousin of Milton Warner, joined and formed a tag team with Luxury Lane. They wore matching karate suits and called themselves *The Luxury Brothers.* Without a doubt, they were an interesting team with differing wrestling techniques. While Charley tried to employ the moves he learned in karate lessons, Jeff used basic wrestling holds. In the meantime, Jim Benson, a friend of Robby Jacobs, also joined the league. Jim didn't enjoy the wrestling show all that much and really only took part due to Rob's wishes. Another newcomer was one of my friends, Mark Fischer, who went by *Fabulous Fischer* and was a hefty kid like ole Matt Denny. So right away, we partnered *Fabulous Fischer* and Matt Denny as a tag team, and their styles fit well together. At this point, Chris "Tuffer" Daniels had left the show after losing interest. All in all, no huge loss, but I liked the "Tuffer" persona and wished Chris had stayed with it.

After doing just a few shows as our announcer, Rob Jacob had seen the fun the rest of us were having wrestling, and he wanted to become a wrestler himself. This concerned me because Rob was so good at the announcing role, and I hated the idea of losing our sole announcer. So after discussing it with Rob, we agreed that he could create a wrestling character called *Jackknife Jacob.* But, he would also continue to announce matches under the name of *Ray Johnson*, which evolved into *Rowdy Ray* in emulation of *Mean Gene Okerlund.* Letting Rob become *Jackknife Jacob* was one of the best decisions I ever made, as the character became one of our league's best all-time villains, meanwhile creating *The Jacob Family* that started a monumental rivalry with the *Crossen/Ackermann Family.* But that is a few chapters ahead—back to where we are at now in this story. Rob's *Jackknife* character was kind of a klutz, but his interview style as a heel was unmatched. He was a lot like Bobby The Brain Heenan, yet in his own way.

Jacknife Jacob debuts in the summer of 1984

During these past few months, our show had been growing considerably. Besides the four cities of Anoka, Champlin, Ramsey, and Andover, we were now being aired in an additional 40 cities near the Minneapolis-St. Paul vicinity. I accomplished this by calling other public access stations throughout the metro area and setting up weekly timeslots. When a show finished running on our cable station, I would send the tape off to another station, and after it was done airing there, then to another station and so on, in order that the show would make it through all the markets for which it was scheduled. To summarize our market reach at this point, *The Kids Quad Cities Pro Wrestling Show* was being seen in Group W Cable's local and regional territories and by subscribers to Storer Cable and Roger Cable Systems, respectively. It really worked out quite well. But while I was taking things more and more seriously, a few others were taking things less seriously, like Milton Warner and Mark Ackermann. They were becoming a problem off-camera. Basically, they were mocking the show, making light of it, and joking around a lot while we were taping. It was as if the show had become a mere joke to them. For those of us who took the show seriously, this was hard to deal with. So Charley and I did our best to just deal with them for the time being.

Ever since we started taping in Group W Cable's studios, I got to know quite a few of the public access employees. People like Dave Nyberg, Pam Hanson, Terry Lovaas, and Scott Tronson. I learned very early on that getting on their *good* side would be very helpful. After all, we have to work under these people to do our show. I actually became good friends with all of them over time. But there was one guy in particular that never liked our show at all, and that was Scott Tronson. He would go out of his way just to give us a hard time. One time, I remember him coming in and shutting off the studio lights while we were taping our final match because we had gone over our timeslot by a mere five minutes. If we were being too loud, he would be the first to barge in while we were taping and yell at us to keep it down. He simply did not like our show, and he took every opportunity to let us know just that.

Fortunately, everyone else working there liked our show, and us, and Scott couldn't make things too difficult all by himself. Terry Lovaas, the public access coordinator at Group W Cable and Scott Tronson's supervisor, became a huge fan of our show. Another guy I got to know real well was Dave Pain, who ran the master control center for all the cable channels, including public access. Being friends with him was important because he could put our show on the air at any time as long as no other programming was scheduled. So as we taped our shows on Saturday mornings, there would be many times I would call Dave and ask him to air our tape unedited so I could preview it live on the air later that day. Befriending *most* of the regular public access staff definitely had its perks.

Shawn Crossen and Mike Ackermann from 1984.

The wrestling show was growing at an encouraging pace, mainly because Charley and I worked well together. What he had, I did not, and vice-versa. I had the ability to organize the show, while Charley managed the existing wrestlers and recruited new ones. In fact, by the end of July, Charley had gotten a few other kids to join. They included Mike Rudnick, who went by *Muscular Mike Rudnick* and had a similar style to that of the late wrestler Brian Pilman, and his tag-team partner Heath Petersen, who went by *Heath Pain Petersen*. The two made a great tag team, and along with Kampa, they became the founding members of *Jackknife Jacob's* tribe, *The Jacob Family*.

Chapter 4
The Shocking News From Charley

Indeed, things were going extremely well for the show with the exposure in 40 different markets in the Twin Cities area. We had even been featured in the *Group W Currier* publication—an in-house magazine sent to cable firm's offices nationwide. The well-written article described Charley and I as the world's youngest cameramen. In addition to the wrestling show, the article explained how Charley and I had been volunteering as cameramen for the Local Origination station, which was the cable company's own channel. Of course, the article also mentioned the *Kids Pro Wrestling Show* that we produced for public access. It was great exposure for all of us, and it was the first of many articles to come that would feature our wrestling show.

Just as things were looking good, however, disaster would strike. And this time, it was a major ordeal. Charley stopped over at my house and told me the shocking news that he and his family would be moving away. At first, I could not believe what I was hearing. "Moving away? To where?" I asked with disbelief. Charley went on to tell me that his dad had been transferred to Omaha, Nebraska, and that they would be moving in less than a month. This was absolutely terrible news—just terrible. I remember the sinking feeling of knowing that my best friend was about to move away. And I knew by the look on Charley's face, that he was feeling the same thing. We did not want to lose that friendship, and it hurt us to know what the reality would be, with him moving nearly 800 miles away. And then there was our wrestling show. What was going to happen to that?

At first, I thought the wrestling show was over. After all, Charley was about to move away. You need to understand that, up until that point, the wrestling show was only in existence due to Charley and myself working together so productively. Like I said earlier, we each brought our own talents to the table. What I did well, Charley lacked. And what Charley had, I did not. So the two of us together were the driving force behind the show. Charley was a true leader and very popular with all the other kids in the show. They admired him and were loyal to him. So at first, I did not know how I could possibly make up for Charley's leadership once he was gone.

But Charley would not let our wrestling show end because of his departure. I remember him pleading with me to keep doing the show, even with him in Omaha. He said it was too important to just end it after all that we had accomplished. Charley then talked to all the other wrestlers and told them that he would be disappointed if any of them would quit just because he was moving away. Charley also advised me that I should consider getting a co-producer or two to help run the show. All of this that he had said and done was extremely important to keeping our show alive during this crucial juncture.

I remember when we taped Charley's final show at Group W Cable. The night before we had a sleepover at my house with Charley, Todd Kampa, Mike Ackermann, Robby Jacob, etc. The sleepover would be our last with Charley for quite awhile, and it served as a fitting going-away tribute to our pal. We had a lot of fun that night as only kids of that age can. During the taping of the show the next day, I remember Charley acting very positive and upbeat when on-camera. But off-camera, the look on his face was of shattered dreams, due to the fact that he did not want to leave the show, and more importantly, our friendship. At the end of the taping, we did a special segment for him, sort of a farewell to Charley. I had all the guys come out and wish him luck on his upcoming move down to Omaha. It was quite an emotional piece for us, and again, Charley maintained his positive attitude while on camera, but afterwards, the look of sheer disappointment washed over his face. This was tough for all of us, and the importance of Charley Lane to our wrestling show shall never be forgotten. He was truly a one-of-a-kind, he really was.

Merciless Mike Ackermann in late 1984.

After Charley moved away, I took his advice and requested help from others in producing the show. I asked Mike Ackermann and Rob Jacob to co-produce with me, they accepted, and the three of us began a very intriguing relationship. Whereas Charley and I worked together like clockwork, the new three-person association did not. Sure, things went well enough at first, but over time I found that we were not all on the same page, especially Rob. Rob could be very stubborn at times, and he had ideas as to what was important and what was not that were different than mine. There would be many times where Rob and I would clash on ideas that we had, and it was really more or less a power struggle between us. But unlike in the past where Charley and I would decide things equally, in this new relationship, I had the final say. This new sense of authority slowly began to consume me, and I am sure that both Mike and Rob found it difficult to work with me at times.

   Mike was easily the more laid-back of the two, and he basically agreed with me on most everything. Mike would do whatever I asked and did it very well. But I must give credit to both Mike and Rob for being hard workers. The three of us labored dutifully with the same goal in mind—to make our show the best it could be. After Charley moved away, my friendship with Mike and Rob grew stronger because of our collaboration on the show. And although Rob and I often clashed, I always valued his dedication and opinions (not all of his ideas were bad ones).

   One of the first things we had to deal in the post-Charley era was Mark Ackermann and Milton Warner. Their constant clowning around was growing thin on all of us. So we had no other choice but to suspend them from the show, or shall we say, kick them out. It all came to a head on Show #13, which was the show following Charley's farewell. Between Mark and Milton, they both kept messing up the end of the show, and I remember how frustrated Mike was getting in the control room. Eventually, he turned to me and asked me if it was OK to get rid of them, and I approved. It was the last time we ever saw Milton Warner on the show. Mark Ackermann would make a special guest appearance later that year on our 25th anniversary show, but that would be it.

The NWF's first lightweight wrestler, The Dynamite Dude.

After those two guys were gone, the show sailed much smoother. Some of the new kids that joined the league were Andy Youngquist, who went by *Andy The Ripper*, Brad Newbolt, ring name *Buster Brad Newbolt*, Marty Bradhoft, known as *Bruiser Bradhoft*, Derek Nash, or *Mad Man Nash*, and his younger brother, Adam Nash, who called himself *The Dynamite Dude*. Adam was our first-ever, true *little league* wrestler. Even though we were all essentially little leaguers, the bigger kids considered themselves to be *heavyweights* on our show. Subsequently, Adam became the NWF's first-ever Lightweight Champion in late 1984. This littlest-of-the-little-league division that Adam started was one I planned to grow.

Chapter 5
Finally, A Wrestling Ring

Sometime back in September of 1984, while walking down the hall of Group W Cable to edit our latest show, I noticed a flyer on the public access bulletin board that advertised a $500 grant. It said to sign up at the office if interested. After considering the idea, I figured that if we were lucky enough to get the grant, we could use the money to transform our wrestling stage into an actual ring by adding four posts and three sets of rope. So I went into the public access office to signup for the grant right away.

As bad luck would have it, I ran into Scott Tronson inside the office and had to ask him for an application for the grant. He replied arrogantly, "Just so you know, there is no guarantee that you guys will get this grant. There are several others lining up for this grant besides you." I thought to myself, *gee really, Scott*? Like I was that ignorant. As Scott handed me the application, I knew he thought we didn't have a snowball's chance in hell of getting the grant. In any event, I filled it out and added it to the stack of other applications. I figured we had nothing to lose in trying.

*A new "wrestling ring" look in late 1984
at Group W Cable studios.*

I kept hoping and praying that we would get the grant, as I visualized how much better our show would look if our "ring" actually had posts and ropes. We all waited a few weeks with our fingers crossed, and then came the news. I remember Terry Lovaas coming up to us at Group W Cable prior to one of our tapings and congratulating us for being awarded the $500 grant. We could not believe it. Both Mike and Rob were speechless. I must admit, I really didn't expect to get that grant either. But now, the rush of actually being awarded the cash was running straight through me. I remember turning to Mike and Rob and saying, "Well, guys, it looks like we are finally going to get that ring after all." I don't remember seeing Scott Tronson after getting the grant. I guess he had more important things to do.

Prior to turning the stage into a ring, I had to configure a way so it could be swiftly assembled before each of our three-hour studio sessions and just as quickly disassembled afterward. So with some advice from my dad, we came up with the idea of attaching four wooden posts to each corner of the stage with large "c" clamps. We then would attach three sets of ropes to the wooden posts using bungee cords as turnbuckles. That was the plan, but I had to inform the owner of the stage and get his permission before going through with the idea. I explained the plan to him over the phone, and he said he thought that it would be fine. So a few days later, we converted the stage into a ring, and our plan worked perfectly but for one small problem. The guy who owned the stage came in as we were finishing up and started bemoaning the fact that we drilled holes into the stage for the "c" clamps. *Was this guy serious?* I thought. Not much could be done at that point. And quite frankly, I didn't care. At last we had a ring! Or, at least something that looks like one.

Our first show with an actual ring (#22, overall) was on October 6th, 1984. While I was editing the show, I was thrilled to see how much more realistic the three ropes and four posts made our production look. Before, all we had was this stage to wrestle on. But now, the ropes and posts made it look like a genuine wrestling ring, and that was extremely important to me. So important, in fact, that I no longer wanted to archive shows previously recorded without the ring—something I would regret years later.

Crusher Crossen with TWA Title Belt in late 1984.

We were now playing in 50-plus cable markets in Minnesota, including the Minneapolis/St. Paul metro area. With this in mind, we changed our show name to the *TWA, Twin Cities Wrestling Association*. I think the actual title was *The Kids Twin Cities Pro Wrestling Show*. A lot of viewers were tuning into our weekly episodes in all the different markets, but our audience was about to increase even more dramatically due to a moment of great publicity. In November of 1984, Elizabeth Child interviewed me for an article in the *Twin Cities Reader* that told our story up to that point in time and ended up inflating our growing fan base across the metro area.

The article's only negative result was perhaps it provided a little too much publicity for us. Shortly after the story was printed, we got a phone call from the other "TWA," *Trans World Airlines*. The airline politely asked us not to use its trademarked initials, TWA, and to change the name of our show. We simply switched our program from TWA to TWF—replacing "Association" with "Federation." To be honest, I was more flattered by our little run-in with a major corporation than anything else.

On the show itself, we had a heated rivalry brewing throughout the summer and fall of 1984 between The Jacob Family and The Crossen/Merciless Family. So it seemed ideal to commemorate our 25th-anniversary show with a high-stakes event that hinged on the two wrestling clans. It was a 10-man, tag-team, elimination-style competition, where the match wore on until the last person left standing represented the winning family. I called this event the *Family Feud Match*, because that's basically what it was at the time. It's interesting to note that I employed this wrestling-event concept nearly four years before Vince McMahon's similarly designed *Survivor Series*. So really, who is copying whom here?

"The Jacob Family" during a 1984 interview with Rich Taylor.

One thing always bugging me was the fact that Ray Johnson could never interview Jackknife Jacob on the show, because needless to say, they were the same person. I remember people in school were giving us a hard time about that, saying, "Who are we really trying to fool?" So on the next show, we used a special effect called "Chrome-Key" that I learned from the studio production class. Chrome-Key essentially allowed Ray Johnson (Rob) to interview Jackknife Jacob (Rob). It took some planning out, as we had to first tape Ray asking the questions before editing an answering Jackknife Jacob into the scene afterwards. And in the end, it was quite mind blowing. It had our friends at school baffled for weeks.

Towards the end of the year, a kid named Rich Taylor joined our league as a color commentator and interviewer. This not only gave Rob a nice break from his Ray Johnson character, but also presented our league with an opportunity to introduce a great friend in Rich to the show. He was a little older than the rest of us, and it showed in terms of his professionalism. Rich was very good at announcing and commentating, and it really helped our show become more professional looking. Rich made a strong impact on the rest of the kids and was very well liked in the show. Other league newcomers included Brian Peterson, who was brought in by Mike Ackermann and went on to become Jackknife Jacob's sidekick. There was also Matt Kelsey, who Rich Taylor dubbed *Kid Kelsey*. Later on, Matt would be known as *Kid USA Kelsey*. Rich Walker joined the league and called himself *Superfly Rich*, because Jimmy Superfly Snuka was his favorite pro wrestler. Rich's brother, Jerry Walker, also joined by the name of *Mr. Wonderful Walker*. I had also recruited my younger cousin, John Fritz, to join the league under the moniker of *Furious Fritz* to help build up the little league division.

The league's new announcer Rich Taylor from late 1984.

Chapter 6
Jacob Quits As The NWF Is Born

As the end of 1984 approached, Rob and I were not getting along. We were wearing thin on each other and arguing over the smallest details. For what it is worth, I thought he was being overly stubborn. Looking back at it now, I realize that I had probably also contributed to our problems. But when Rob said he was missing our next taping (#32) without an excuse, I suspended him for five shows. At that time, we actually issued *real* suspensions for disciplinary reasons. The suspensions would normally be announced on the show, so of course, no one liked getting suspended.

Rob Jacob aka "Jackknife Jacob" from late 1984.

Rob felt I was being totally unfair to him with the suspension, and he said he was going to quit the show. I told him fine, and I then informed him that he would never be allowed back. It was a bitter break-up, and to this day, it remains one of my biggest regrets with the show. You see, at the time, I had let the show go to my head. And firing Rob was a huge mistake. As a co-producer, announcer, and wrestler, he had always given everything he had to the show. His Ray Johnson character had always been important to the show, and his Jackknife Jacob character was nearly irreplaceable. Yet at the time, I just did not see any of that. Instead, because of my ego, I felt that getting rid of him was the right thing to do.

During the next taping at Group W Cable, Rich Taylor announced the suspension and firing of Rob Jacob. And during many of the wrestlers' interviews, we took mean-spirited cracks at Rob. Even his protégée, Brian Peterson, had a few choice words for him. And not only was Rob watching all of this when it aired, but so was the rest of the school and metro area for that matter. I cannot imagine what it must have felt like to have to deal with all of that. Looking back at it now, we surely had to have hurt Rob's feelings with our remarks on that show. For all he did for our league—and this was how we thanked him? But in our defense, we were kids being kids, and obviously acting like it. However, if I failed to say it plainly enough at the time, let me say it now: My deepest apologies, Rob.

Right after Rob left, a few major things began happening with the show. I figured if I could successfully distribute the show to the Twin Cities cable markets, then why not do it nationwide? So with that idea in mind, I spent a few days calling up every major cable market in the top cities all across the country and started setting up weekly timeslots. Once I had the slots, it was only a matter of mailing the tapes to each market each week. And with those phone calls, I picked up nearly 20 major cities—New York, Los Angeles, Miami, Denver, Chicago, Atlanta, and Dallas, to name a few. Unfortunately, I didn't realize I was running up a pretty hefty phone bill that would later dishearten my parents.

Original NWF logo design from early 1985.

So now that we we're airing our show nationwide, on show #33, Rich Taylor announced that we were to be known as the *NWF, the National Wrestling Federation*. It was around this time that we set up our NWF hotline, where viewers could call in to either join the league or leave us comments. I would also set up special guest messages from our wrestlers on the hotline. And, up to this point in time, all of us kids were handling the entire batch of studio duties—from directing in the control room to running the cameras. But I wanted to concentrate more on running the wrestling show in general, so I put together a production crew of public access volunteers. It worked out well, and my title on the show was now "Executive Producer." I had the crew take care of all the technical aspects of the show, while I oversaw the entire production.

Matt Kelsey recruited Andrew Karlsen to become a wrestler in early 1985. At first, Andrew wrestled as a Russian in a mask. But later, he got rid of the mask and became known as *Ace*. Matt Kelsey's younger brother, Ryan Kelsey, became *Rough Ryan* for our little league division. Matt Kelsey also recruited a pair of twins named Todd and Troy Dusosky, who were known in the ring as *The Super Ds*. Mike Ackermann brought in a guy named Chuck Roberts, who ended up going by *Roughhouse Roberts*. On the opposite side of things, 1984 marked the end of the careers for the likes of *Bruiser Bradhoft*, *Andy the Ripper Youngquist*, and *Mr. Wonderful Walker* as they all became less interested in the wrestling show. And in early 1985, our favorite announcer, Rich Taylor, had decided to leave the show. I liked Rich a lot and wished he had stayed with us.

Ace wins the NWF World Title in early 1985.

Although most NWF matches had been predetermined, the outcomes of the title bouts still went unscripted at this point in time. Basically, the outcomes were real in that the only way to claim victory would be with a pin—or in the case of show #34, where one opponent allows the other to win. During show #34, I decided to let Ace defeat me for the World Title. I felt allowing Ace to hold the title was the right thing to do for the league at the time because it made things more interesting for the fans as it was surely unexpected. Also, championing Ace enhanced both his "heel" persona and general reputation as a wrestler. I might have lost the title, but it was a win-win situation for the league.

It was February of 1985, when Charley Lane called me and said he was in town for the weekend. I was so excited. I told him I would immediately meet him halfway from where he was staying, a few blocks away at his relative's house. When we spotted each other down the street, we ran as fast as we could to one another and hugged in pure joy. We were so happy to see each other again after not seeing each other for the past six months. I will never forget that moment. That night, I showed Charley several tapes of the wrestling show, and he was impressed with our new ring. The next day, Show #35 was taped featuring the return of non other than Luxury Lane (Charley). We also set up a "battle royal" for the main event, and I felt it was only fitting that Charley was allowed to win it. Charley enjoyed making his special guest appearance back on the show. And as he left back for Omaha, he reminded me he would be back for Easter weekend again.

Luxury Lane wins the main event battle royal in 1985.

With all the publicity from the *Twin Cities Reader* article we received a few months back, I thought that perhaps the local news stations might be interested in running a story about our league as well. So I proceeded to contact the three major stations in the Twin Cities, they were *KSTP-TV, WCCO-TV*, and *WUSA-TV*. I contacted the sports room news desks at each of them and told them about our league. I referred to the *Twin Cities Reader* article as reference material for them to look into for more information about us. Out of the three, the only one that showed any interested was *KSTP-TV*, Channel 5. I was given to a guy by the name of Larry Burnett, who was one of their local sports reporters. He liked the idea of doing a story and said he would get back to us soon.

Just as things were looking better than ever with the show, once again, disaster would strike. When I booked the studio for our next taping on March 16th, 1985, Scott Tronson told me that he had some bad news. He said that this would have to be our last show using the wooden stage/ring in the studio. I said, "What! What are you talking about?" He went on to say that they made a decision to get rid of the wooden stage we were using because it was taking up too much space. I was absolutely furious. Scott went on to suggest that maybe we could prop up our posts using bricks to support them or something like that. Yeah sure, Scott, that would work *real* well. What a lame thing to say. Not only was I mad, but I was also scared as to what was going to happen to our show.

So, there we sat: We just had a nice article written about us in the *Twin Cities Reader*; we had over 70 cable markets both locally and nationally all expecting weekly shows from us; we had a local news station that was about to do a story on our league; and now, our show was at the brink of destruction due to not having a wrestling ring. I was not about to go backwards and go without a ring again—that was simply not even an option. The only solution was to find a new place to tape our show from where we could have a wrestling ring again, but where?

Chapter 7
A New Beginning

After Scott Tronson dropped that bombshell on us, I spent days trying to think up a solution. Of course, the Fred Moore boxing ring crossed my mind. But Mr. Daniels had already said no to that idea a year ago, so what would make him think any different now? I was sure Tronson thought that this was going to be the end of our weekly wrestling show, but I was not about to quit over this. I kept thinking and thinking every day. I figured there had to be an answer to this—there just had to be.

I was in our family garage a few days later, and I noticed how the garage ceiling was actually finished. Then, it hit me … I could transform our garage into a studio and build a ring inside the garage! The thought was perfect! Right off the bat, I could visualize it. But before I got too excited, I knew I had to first get my mom's permission. I went on to tell her about my idea, and at first she thought I was crazy, but after a bit of prying and conning on my part, she finally caved in and said all right. Looking back, she knew how hard I had worked on the wrestling show, and she knew it was keeping us kids out of trouble. Boy, was I lucky to have parents that trusted me in what I was doing with our wrestling show. Because most parents would never let their kids build a ring and run a wrestling federation—let alone in their garage.

With my mom's approval secured, Mike Ackermann and I came up with a design for the new ring. We decided to build one that would be 12 ft. x 12 ft. and 12 inches off the ground (due to the somewhat low ceiling in the garage). We were able to utilize the posts and ropes from the ring in the old studio, and we had some spare lumber in the garage. But we still were going to need about $250-worth of lumber and additional materials. I had been saving up my allowance at the time, so I used that and some money from my parents on loan to purchase the needed materials.

Mad Man Nash parts ways with Merciless Mike in early 1985.

In the meantime, we still had our final show to tape in Group W Studios. I decided to do two tapings that day to free up the following week, so we could prepare the new studio and build a ring in my garage. During those final Group W Cable sessions, two things happened involving Mike Ackermann that I remember very well to this day. The first concerned Mike's World Title belt aspirations. Yes, Mike was not only in line for a title shot against *Ace* but convinced that he would beat him. So when *Mad Man Nash* announced that he was dropping Mike as his partner and joining Peterson's Family (while picking *Killer Kampa* as his new partner), Mike just blew it off because he planned to take the World Title from *Ace* on that day. Well, Mike got his match with *Ace*. But the one thing Mike did not plan for was how small the ring was in the studio. Every time Mike would get *Ace* in a pinning situation, *Ace* would grab the ropes, and the hold had to be broken. This went on and on, until eventually, the time limit expired. Mike did not win the belt, and I had never seen him so mad as he was afterwards. He was so upset that he literally stomped out of the ring and disappeared for nearly an hour. He was *very* ticked off. But to *Ace's* credit, grabbing the ropes was a smart thing to do, as he knew he was outmatched, so it was his only defense.

The second thing that happened was in Mike's match with Brian Peterson on the second taping that day. As I said before, Brian was very aggressive in the ring. And during this match, he took a metal folding chair and hit Mike pretty hard on the head. It ended up giving Mike a concussion. So as a result of that incident, we put in a new rule that any use of folding chairs on your opponent would result in an immediate suspension. So for a long time thereafter, there were no more chairs used in matches, where prior to this, it was beginning to be a regular occurrence on the show.

Brian Peterson give Merciless Mike a concussion
from a chair shot.

After our last taping at Group W Studios, the next thing we had to do was clean out my parents' garage to make room for the new studio. So a few of the guys and I got together and went to work. Once that was done, we started to build our ring. We had to build it in three sections so that it could be set up and taken down when we were not using it, so that my mom could park her car in the garage. We had a pretty good-sized garage; it was about 28 ft. x 28 ft. Our ring size of 12 ft. x 12 ft. would fit inside it pretty nicely.

As we were completing the ring, I decided to replace the bungee cord turnbuckles with real metal turnbuckles, so that we could tighten up the ropes just like on a real ring. This made the ropes actually work now. So with that, you could climb on top of them and actually run into them and hit them just like in a real ring. The last thing we did was hang up several blue plastic tarps on all the walls inside the garage, so that it would not look like a garage when we start taping the wrestling shows.

Ring posts now using actual turnbuckles
in new ring design from 1985.

I remember shortly after finishing the ring, a few of my friends in the neighborhood stopped by to check out the new ring we built.

I mentioned how we can actually hit the ropes now, and I proceeded to demonstrate how it worked. I started running back and forth as fast as I could hitting the ropes each time when all of a sudden … *crack!* One of the wooden posts completely broke in half as I hit the ropes, and I went flying out of the ring landing in my nearby beer can collection outside the ring. Everyone started laughing, and I was a bit embarrassed as I recall. But one thing I knew for certain, the wooden posts would have to go. Within a few weeks, we replaced them with steel posts, which I got from my dad from the factory he worked at.

We did our first taping in the garage on April 6th, 1985. And what a day that turned out to be. First of all, Charley was back in town again. I remember how impressed he was with what we did to our garage, as far as turning it into a wrestling studio, so to speak. And it was great to have him make a guest appearance on the show again. Also on that show, I was involved in a six-man tag team match. During the match, I had Mike in a "Boston Crab" hold. And then, Chuck Roberts decided to jump on my back. Well, you can guess what happened next. I went face first into the mat with all of Robert's weight on top of me. As a result, my front tooth went through my bottom lip, blood was everywhere, and this time it was *real*. As far as my bottom lip, it was nasty looking and one of the worst injuries that I had ever experienced.

Also, this is the show that had the very controversial title match between Chuck Roberts and *Ace*. If you watch the match, Chuck Roberts actually pins *Ace* in the middle of the ring. However, the following week on the show, the title was returned back to *Ace*. What gives here? Can you say, *politics*? Right after Chuck won the match, I immediately went into the ring and tried to get the referee to reverse his decision. I remember Roberts noticing me in the ring, and he shouted, "So, you're not the ref, Shawn," as he knew what I was up to. When that failed, I pleaded with Chuck off camera to agree to let *Ace* have the title back due to poor officiating. And after a few days of me pleading to him, he agreed. But to be honest with you, he shouldn't have. After all, he did win that belt fair and square.

*New ring design featuring normal steel posts
and turnbuckle padding.*

Also, there were some fresh faces on this show. Allison Givins, a good friend from the neighborhood, had asked me if she could be a guest commentator. She was a tomboy and into sports, so I said, sure, why not. This was the first time we ever had a girl on the show, and she did well. Also, Mike mentioned that a kid who had previously called on the hotline would be joining us. He turned out to be Steve Engstrom, who was a bit older than the rest of us at the age of 16. And when he showed up, he surprised us all with a very cool costume for his character. He had an all-white suit with a white mask with a black "X" on the forehead; he said he wanted to call himself *Mr. X*. I have to admit, it was a great concept and character, and I was very impressed with the efforts he made in preparing for the show. But this guy would be full of surprises as time went on. If I only knew what the future would bring with Steve Engstrom ... but I will let that story tell itself.

The first taping in the garage studio was planned and executed really well. The only bad thing was my bottom lip, which swelled up like a prune later that night. I remember my mom wanted to take me to Mercy Medical Center for stitches. I had known about getting stitches all too well from previous experiences, and I was deathly against that idea. But that aside, I was just glad to know that we had beaten the odds again and were back on the track of making wrestling shows again.

Chapter 8
The Ups And Downs
On The Road To Success

As we started regularly producing wrestling shows from our family garage, I started to get to know Steve Engstrom very well, and he was turning out to be quite the handyman around the new studio. He made innovative technical improvements to our wrestling ring and produced other helpful ideas. For instance, he took it upon himself to enhance the look of the World Title belt. I mean, this belt actually looked like the real deal. Prior to Steve's alterations, our title belt was made out of wood with sheet metal over it, but this new one had actual shiny chrome metal plates, with all sorts of decals and emblems on it. The new title belt was very attractive looking. I found Steve's talents to be very helpful and impressive.

Wouldn't you know only after taping a couple shows in the garage that good ole Scott Tronson would manage to interfere with our production? As I look back at it now, he must have been pretty disappointed with how we managed to keep the NWF running. So stooping as low as he could go, he wound up suspending us from checking out the public access equipment because of "profanity." As it turns out, one of the wrestlers during his after-match interview stated that he was "pissed." And according to Scott, "pissed" was a swear word that you could not say on the air. *You have to be kidding me*? I thought. What would this guy think of next? Well, the suspension was only for two weeks, so no big deal really. But the nerve of this guy—you'd think he would have better things to do with his time, wouldn't you?

Things with Mike and myself were not going too well. I don't know if it was the fact that I was getting buddy-buddy with the new kid, Steve, and not giving Mike as much attention, or what. But Mike and I were starting to get very short with each other. It had started out with little things that were said back and forth. But every time those small things occurred, our problems with each other seemed to be getting bigger and bigger. There were things I wanted to do that Mike would not agree with, and vice-versa. Where we once had a solid working relationship, now it seemed as though we were always at each other's throats. In the end, we made a concerted effort to tolerate each other.

During one of our regular tapings in May of 1985, Larry Burnett from KSTP-TV Channel 5 finally came out to our garage studio to do his story for the evening news. We were all excited. I remember him showing up at the garage with a cameraman. They filmed us doing a match from beginning to end, and then they interviewed several kids one-on-one, myself included. They must have spent a good hour with us. Larry even did a separate interview with us on our own show, which I thought was really cool of him. Well, later that night, we all watched the news with eager anticipation and were shocked to see our story highlighted for the sports segment, as the station had a preview of the piece before a commercial break. The segment itself could not have been done any better, as it really showcased our league very well. It also turned out to be great publicity for us. I remember going to school the next day and hearing everyone talk about it, and I do mean *everyone*. We sent Larry Burnett a "Thank You" card that we all signed. I felt it was the right thing to do.

NWF featured on the Eyewitness News sports update in 1985.

It was right after this that Mike and I finally had it out. And once again, I let my big mouth do something that I end up regretting for years to come—I fired Mike from the show. When you are 15 years old, and you have had all the success that our league has had, you think that it is all because of you. And while that may have been partially true, it was also people like Mike who helped make the whole thing successful with good old-fashioned elbow grease and creativity. But like an idiot, I just could not see that then. So with that, after getting in a heated argument with Mike over our next taping, I fired him from the show, and that was the last time I had a co-producer again. At that point, I would create a *producers council*, where I would have a group of kids help run the show but without the authority of a co-producer. I guess you could consider the *producers council* similar to a *board of directors*, if you will.

We continued to tape shows throughout the summer of 1985, and things on the show just kept getting better and better. Steve kept making several improvements to our wrestling ring. At first, it was 12 ft. x 12 ft., then he made it bigger to 13.5 ft. x 13.5 ft., and then it went to 15 ft. x 15 ft. Steve added a blue tarp for the canvas of the ring. Steve also upgraded our turnbuckles by adding colorful pads. After Mike left, I spent a lot of time with Steve in getting to know him, and he was really turning out to be a great guy. I asked him to be on the producers council along with Matt Kelsey, who I had became pretty good friends with since he joined as well, and they both graciously accepted the offer.

From the fans' perspective, that summer had some of the best shows we ever produced as far as character development was concerned. We had a huge diversity on the roster, and our little league division had just as many wrestlers as our heavyweight division. We had so many kids on the show, that in those days, when you were not wrestling, you became part of the studio audience, which added a nice touch to the show. Todd Chester, who called himself *Todd The Bodd*, was one of the kids who joined that summer. His tag team partner, Chuck Roberts, recruited him, and they would become the famous NWF tag team, *The Ring Warriors*. Chad Johnson also joined, calling himself *Jumpin' Johnson*, with his partner *Dr. B*, both recruited by Andrew Karlsen. Josh Jungling joined up, calling himself *Jungle Man Josh*, as brought in by Derek Nash. Steve also had a few new guys, such as Tim Holland, known as *Thandar*, and his cousin, Troy Otto, who became *Bull Dog Butcher*. As far as little leaguers, we had Dean Karlsen, the younger brother of Andrew (*Ace*), Chad Reinholtz, calling himself *Rock-n-Roll Reinholtz*. Then there was *The Bunes Brothers*, Troy and Brian Bunes, recruited by Andrew Karlsen. In addition to Steve's *Mr. X character*, he asked if he could do a new character without the mask and called himself *Pretty Boy Taylor*. He wanted to be a Texan-type character, and I thought it sounded like a great idea, so I said sure.

Steve debuts his new character "Pretty Boy Taylor" in 1985.

Shortly thereafter, I learned something shocking about Steve. He had started to talk to my older sisters regularly, and we all eventually learned that Steve was not 16 years old. In fact, he was 26 years old! To make matters even more surprising, he was married with two young kids as well. We were all shocked. And at first, I didn't believe it. But then Steve showed me his driver's license, and I knew he was telling the truth. I asked him why he lied about his age, and he replied, "Because I knew you would not let me join the show if I told you the truth." And he was absolutely right on that. He then went on to say, "But now I figured I showed you what I can do to help, and I really like the wrestling show a lot, so if you want me, then great, I will stay. But if you don't want me, I will understand that too." What can you say to that? I mean, in those past few months, he did more to improve our show than anyone I could have imagined. How could I possibly get rid of this guy now? And even though he lied to us, I just did not have the heart to get rid of him—not after all he had done for us. So with that, Steve was our one exception to our age limit on the show.

So as the summer came to a close, it was a successful one for our show. We were still being broadcast in over 70 percent of the Twin Cities cable markets, as well as some twenty cities nationwide, each and every week. The NWF Kids Pro Wrestling Show was growing in popularity. And our actual wrestling moves were getting better and better as well. Our matches were starting to look pretty good, as we were doing most all of the normal moves that were being done in the pros at the time. And we were coming up on our 50th anniversary show, which was just around the corner. For this show, I was planning on some special things to do.

Chapter 9
Fifty Shows, A Title Match,
And Nowhere To Go

Just prior to our 50th show, two important things happened. The first one was Matt Kelsey (*Kid USA Kelsey*) pinned Andrew Karlsen (*Ace*) for the NWF World Title on Show #48. This was a huge upset, as Andrew had defended against Kelsey several times before and had always maintained his title. The other item was a title match for the NWF Lightweight belt, as Adam Nash (*The Dynamite Dude*) defended against Ryan Kelsey (*Rough Ryan*). Now as I said before, our title matches were never predetermined, and the only way to win was by a pinfall, or submission. So during the title match, Adam got Ryan in a "camel clutch" and never let go. None of us knew it at the time, but Ryan could not breathe while in this hold by Adam. And the referee could not tell that anything was wrong. After a minute or so, Ryan somehow managed to submit, and Adam released his hold on Ryan. But as Ryan started to catch his breath, he was in tears.

A shocked "Ace" loses his NWF Title Belt to "Kid Kelsey" in 1985.

He was mainly scared because he could not breathe, and Adam had no intention to actually hurt him—it was just one of those fluke things. But Adam felt terrible for what he had done to Ryan, as I remember Adam trying to comfort Ryan outside the ring immediately following the match. Ryan was a bit shook up, but he would bounce back the following week. Adam, on the other hand, was another story. That incident scared him, as he felt totally responsible for what he did to Ryan. Adam blamed himself and felt extremely guilty for what he did and what could have happened to Ryan. And despite several attempts on my part to get him not to do it, he ended up quitting the NWF for good.

On August 24th, 1985, we were taping our 50th show, which we called the *NWF's 50th Anniversary Show Special*. To commemorate the show, I decided to invite some of the older kids that used to be on the show to come back and make a special appearance. And a few accepted, such as Mike Rudnick, Keith Wiltermouth, Todd Kampa, and Brian Peterson. Also, I had really missed having both Mike Ackermann and Rob Jacob on the show. I never felt good about the way I got rid of them to begin with. So knowing I had done wrong, I wrote them both letters expressing my deepest apologies and asking them to come back to the show. I put a lot into those two letters, and I hoped that they would accept my apologies. I then called each of them, and Rob said he appreciated my apology, however, he had decided that he did not want to return to the NWF. I then called Mike, and after talking a bit, he said he had decided that he would return to the show. I was happy that at least one of them accepted my offer. I wished Rob had thought differently as well, but what else could I do at that point?

But over the next week or so, Mike would change his mind and decide not to come back after all. I could never understand that. What made him change his mind I thought? Did Rob have something to do with Mike's change of heart? I guess I'll never know. But I was really hurt when Mike went back on his word, but I respected his decision. All I knew was I made peace with both of them by apologizing to them and inviting them back to the show. But as it is, they both ended up choosing to stay out of the league. What more could I do? Besides, simply telling them both I was sorry was the important thing, and I felt much better about the whole situation after doing that.

Our 50th show was a two-hour special, and with all the returning kids, along with our current regulars, this show ended up being one of our more entertaining productions. In fact, all four of them (Rudnick, Wiltermouth, Kampa, and Peterson) ended up asking to stay in the league after the 50th show, which I had no problems with at all. This did end up being Andrew Karlsen's final show, however. The week prior, Andrew had lost his NWF World Title belt to Matt Kelsey, and so on the 50th show, *Ace* got his rematch. However, he was not successful in the rematch, and with that, he ended up quitting the NWF for good after that second loss to Kelsey. Although I made several attempts for the next six months to get him to return, he chose to stay out of the league and pursue his other interests.

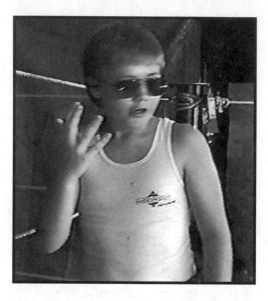

Jason Clauson joins the league as
"Corporal Clauson" from late 1985.

Shortly after the 50th show, a few new wrestlers entered the NWF. Matt Kelsey brought in one kid, Jason Clauson. At first he was a wrestler by the name of *Corporal Clauson*, but behind the scenes, he ended up doing some commentating during other matches. Afterwards, when I was editing the show and I was able to hear Jason's announcing style, I knew right then and there that we had found ourselves a new announcer. Another kid I brought in was Troy Steenerson, who I named *Slick Steenerson*. Troy was a big-sized kid, but he could throw a mean drop kick for a kid his size, which was pretty impressive to say the least.

After the 50th show, quite a few of the wrestlers ended up quitting, and I never understood why. But all of the following were now gone from the league: Troy and Brian Bunes, Eric Balabon, Derek and Adam Nash, Chad Johnson, Chad Reinholtz, and Dean Karlsen. Most of the guys quit because Andrew Karlsen had recruited them, so that did not surprise me. But the two that did catch me off-guard were Adam and Derek Nash. Both of them had been in the show since the summer of 1984, and they had really good characters on the show. I guess I could see Adam's point with what happened to Ryan in that title match, but Derek was a complete surprise. I really missed those two after they left, because they each had brought unique and talented personalities to our show.

On November 16th, 1985, I was next in line for a title shot against Matt Kelsey. Now Matt and myself were good friends both in and out of the ring. But going into this match, deep down, I really wanted that title belt. I told Matt the week prior that, all friendships aside, when that bell rings, I would be coming for that belt with everything I got, "so please let us not have any hard feelings afterwards." And he agreed. So the bell rings, and we trade a few moves back and forth for the first few minutes. And about four minutes in, I make my move. I figured if I could get Matt in a leg scissors and squeeze as hard as I can, he would submit. So that's what I did. But to my surprise, Matt would not give up. He was screaming at the top of his lungs in pain shouting, "Never! Never!" After several minutes of this, Matt was in tears, mainly from his rage. Still, he was in a battle for survival, that much I knew. After a while, my legs started to get sore from the pressure I was applying, and I could not have imagined what Matt was feeling. I remember I heard the announcers at ringside saying that there were only two minutes remaining in our match, and I knew that my time was running out. So, I switched gears and went for a pin. At that point, Matt was just too worn out, and I managed to pin him. I did it! Crusher Crossen had won the title back for the fourth time. But as I was celebrating in the ring, a defeated Matt Kelsey was in pain while lying on the ring apron below.

Crossen and Kelsey battle it out for the NWF title in 1985.

It was great to win the title, as I really wanted to win it back. But at the same time, I did not want to hurt my friendship with Matt, and he was hurt both physically and emotionally. Matt would not speak to me for several weeks after this match. I felt bad, as I did not mean to hurt his feelings like I did. I remember I tried calling him at home, and he would not take the calls. He avoided me in the halls at school as well. This went on for weeks. And it was then that I decided that title matches would no longer be for real, as all of our friendships were more important than that. So that match ended up being the last title match that was for real, from then on all outcomes in title matches were predetermined. After a few weeks had passed, I had my first interview as champion during a taping of our *Monday Night Madness Show* with Brian Balabon, when Matt came out and interrupted the interview. He shook my hand and congratulated me on winning the title from him. You have to understand that while Matt did this, he did it in front of everyone in our league, his family at home, and everyone else watching our show on cable TV. And that took a lot for Matt to do that, as he swallowed his pride *big time*. Whether you were a fan of Kelsey or not, you had to be impressed with him after that. Doing what he did was nothing short of a class act, plain and simple. And although we became friends again, it would never be the same. That match had permanently damaged a part of our friendship, forever.

Cable TV let Shawn Crossen, 15, produce his own TV show. Stations will do the same for you even if you have little money or talent.

If a kid can start his own TV show, so can you
By Steven Kaplan

Minneapolis Star and Tribune article on the NWF from late 1985.

In December of 1985, we once again got a break with publicity as the *Minneapolis Star Tribune* wrote a beautiful article on our show, which was featured in the weekend magazine section of the Sunday paper. This was a huge piece for us, as the *Star Tribune* was a huge paper, covering the entire state of Minnesota with millions of readers. But the article had one sour note to it. As bad luck would have it, our family insurance agent who provided my parent's homeowners insurance had also read the article. And when he reads the part about us using the garage, that's all she wrote. The next thing I know is we can no longer use the garage or else this insurance agent would cancel our homeowner's insurance policy on the entire property. A million questions were racing through my mind. Where were we going to wrestle now? What was going to happen to our show? What about my weekly commitments all around the country for our wrestling show? Had we finally reached the end of our wrestling show?

Chapter 10
Where There's A Will, There's A Way

So as 1985 comes to a close, the future of the NWF looked about as grim as it could get. The garage studio that we were using for the past ten months was now no longer available due to this insurance agent. Right after my mom had told me this news, I immediately called up the insurance agent myself. I don't remember exactly what was said, but I do remember hanging up on him towards the end of the call. So the bottom line was we needed a new place to do our wrestling shows, plain and simple.

Just prior to getting this news about losing the use of our garage, I had asked Jason Clauson to join the NWF *producers council.* Jason had natural leadership abilities in my opinion. Jason was honored to be a part of the NWF team. And as I got this news regarding the garage, I shared it with Jason to see if he had any ideas. At first, we could not come up with anything. But the first issue at hand was taking care of our weekly show timeslots. And we did this by filming special *Monday Night Madness* shows in its place. The *Monday Night Madness* show was basically a recap show with interview segments and highlights of prior matches. So in our spare time, Jason, and I continued to try to think up a solution as far as where we could tape new wrestling shows from.

I told Jason about the ring in the basement of Fred Moore Jr. High School, and how Mr. Daniels, the community school director at Fred Moore, had said no to the idea roughly two years prior. And Jason suggested I try talking to someone higher up the ladder instead of Mr. Daniels. That was a good point, as I had never thought of doing it before. So I went to the principle at Fred Moore, Mr. Lerom. I explained our situation, and he suggested I speak to Mr. Stewart at the school district headquarters. Mr. Stewart was in charge of all community school activities for the entire school district, and he basically was Mr. Daniels' boss. So I spoke to Mr. Stewart and explained our situation to him. And I would never forget his exact words, he said, "I don't see why this should be a problem. Let me speak to Mr. Daniels, and we will get back to you on this." It certainly sounded hopeful, so we all kept our fingers crossed as we waited in anticipation over the next several days.

Shawn Crossen and Jason Clauson from early 1986.

In the meantime, I explained to Jason that I was not happy with the way the last few shows went from the garage. They were very unorganized, and a lot of the kids were clowning around and not taking the show very seriously, and that bothered me. So with that, Jason and myself ended up releasing many of the kids from the show who were causing problems, and they included Todd Kampa, Keith Wiltermouth, and Brian Peterson. With that, I explained to Jason that I also wanted to get more new wrestlers to join the show as well, so for the months of December and into January of 1986 during every week on our make-shift shows, we started pushing our NWF recruiting segments where we encouraged kids from the surrounding communities to call up the NWF Hotline and join the league.

Not more than a week after talking to Mr. Stewart from the school district headquarters, I ended up getting a note in class to see Mr. Daniels in his office at Fred Moore. At first, Mr. Daniels was upset that I did not come to him first with the request to use the boxing ring in the basement, he said something like, "What you did was wrong, you should have done things in the right steps, and come to me first instead of going over my head." Then, he went on to say that we would be given a six-month pilot starting in January of 1986 to use the ring at Fred Moore Jr. High, as long as the following requirements were met. One, we needed an adult supervisor on hand at all times while we used of the ring. Two, we needed Golden Gloves Boxing's permission to use the ring. He then reminded us that this was only a pilot, and that the period would be reviewed after six months to see if we could continue permanently. As far as Mr. Daniels' concerns about us going over his head, I wanted to tell him, "We did ask you two years ago, and you said no." But what good would that do bringing it up in the first place? So I just let it go.

I was so happy to have finally gotten into Fred Moore to use their boxing ring. Once again, we dodge another bullet and keep the wrestling show alive. I remember I called Jason to tell him the news. He was excited and relieved, as we were all on pins and needles that week waiting for the school's response. Referring to Mr. Daniels' concerns, I remember Jason telling me, "You should have told him that we did do things in the right steps, we just *stepped* on you." Jason was always good for a laugh or two, and we both laughed over that for quite some time. But the best part was, we were about to start taping regular wrestling shows again, and that was a great feeling for all of us.

Around this time, I also got an interesting phone call from a local production company in town. They had read the article in the *Minneapolis Star Tribune* a few weeks back, and invited my parents and I out for dinner to discuss some ideas they had. We met at The Green Mill restaurant in Minneapolis, and during that dinner, they asked me all sorts of questions. Why did I start the wrestling show? What makes it fun? What do I like about it? What don't I like about it? What are my goals with it? What are my dreams with it? Honestly, I had never been asked such questions before, it was quite mind blowing. In the end, they said they were interested in producing an *After School Special* on my life and what I had done with the wrestling show. They said that nothing was for certain, and that they were only looking into this idea. I guess I was flattered to think that my story was that interesting to them. I mentioned to them that we were planning on doing our first taping out of Fred Moore in just a few weeks, and they asked if they could attend that taping to do further research on our show, so I said sure.

Mr. X does a superfly death leap
onto Steenerson from Fred Moore.

On January 25th, 1986, we taped our first show from the Fred Moore Jr. High Basement using the Golden Gloves Boxing ring. Our first taping was actually an event that was originally planned to take place back in December from our garage studio, but obviously it had to be postponed. That event was called *Superstars Spectacular '85*. We had plenty of new wrestlers on the show that day as well. Jason Clauson had recruited a pair of brothers named Steve and Jim Owens to be our new Russian tag team, as they were called *The Russian Destroyers*. Also, Jason brought in Peter Nguyen, and his character was called *The Tokyo Terror*. Peter was actually a Vietnamese kid, but since nobody from our age really understood the Vietnam War, having him play a Japanese wrestler made much more sense to us, so we had him as being from Japan. Also, we had several new wrestlers who had joined through our NWF hotline over the past month, and they included Tony, who went by the name *Tough Tony* and was our first Russian little leaguer, Chad Ronnebaum, who called himself *Rock-n-Ronnebaum*, Chris Eyrich, who went by wrestling name of *The Eye*, Chris Hanson, who at first was called *The Masher* and was one half of *The Rough Russians*, but by the following week, he would do a complete turnabout, as he became *Sergeant Smash* from the good ole USA.

Crossen suplexes Taylor from Fred Moore in 1986.

The show went well, and the environment at Fred Moore was perfect. The league was really on a roll now that we had all these new wrestlers and a game plan that seemed to be working. We had use of the ring at Fred Moore every week, so one week we would tape two shows for cable, and then on the following week, we would practice our wrestling moves during practice sessions. This way, we were able to teach the kids how to do the moves correctly, so that no one would get hurt. It really worked well, and it also improved the quality of our matches over time. The guys from that production company showed up at our first show like they said they would, and they took notes and several pictures while we did our show. But in the end, they never went any further with their *After School Special* production. It's sort of funny looking back at that production company now, because the last thing they asked me at that dinner was if I could have anything I wanted for the show, what would it be? And I told them that I wished I could have a live event in some arena type setting in front of a real audience with multiple cameras filming the entire show, and do it just like the big time leagues do. And the funny thing about that is, that dream was about to become a reality in just a few short months to come.

Chapter 11
The Anoka Armory

At the start of 1986, things were going very well for our wrestling show. We had just gotten into Fred Moore Jr. High and were able to use their boxing ring every Saturday morning, we had new kids joining the show in record numbers, and Jason and myself were really working well together as a team. As I had discussed with Matt, Steve, and Jason earlier on at the beginning of the year, I really wanted to improve the wrestling abilities of all the other kids. What I mean is, Steve and myself were probably the best at doing the moves at the time, and I wanted the rest of the kids playing on the same level as us. Jason agreed strongly on this, and so on the Saturdays that we were not taping a show, we took those practice sessions very seriously. We would show all the kids how to take basic falls, veil throws, and hip tosses. We would show them how to do the basic body slams, leg drops, and clotheslines. I remember I would set up extra pads in the ring and have all the kids learn the flying drop kick by using the extra padding to land on. And I must admit, these practice sessions did pay off after doing a few of them, as the matches were looking better and better as far as the moves went.

After school, Jason, Matt, and myself would often meet at Hans Bakery, which was a little donut shop right across the street from Fred Moore. After a few donuts, we would usually chum around downtown Anoka and just hang out. And, it was on a day such as this (and I remember it well) that the three of us left Hans Bakery and walked down 5th Avenue towards Main Street. As we got to the corner of 5th and Main, we turned down Main Street passing the Anoka Movie Theater, and then the next building was the Anoka Armory. And there was a sign out front advertising an upcoming gun show, and as we passed that sign and I stared off at the building, the old light bulb went off in my head and the idea hit me. What if we held a live event here at the Anoka Armory? So I stopped, told Matt and Jason my idea, and they both laughed it off. Once they knew I was not joking, immediate concern washed over Jason's face while Matt thought I was simply crazy. But I convinced them both to go inside with me to investigate the possibilities to see if it could even be done.

After getting a tour of the facilities and meeting with the senior drill sergeant on duty, I was absolutely convinced we were going to be able to do this. It was perfect. They had a huge open floor area complete with folding chairs that would seat 450 people. They had private dressing rooms, a concession area, and restrooms as well as showers. And during that tour, I immediately could visualize us holding a live card in that building. After talking to the sergeant, he explained that we needed to come up with a down payment of $100 to reserve a date and then $350 to rent the building per day. And I was sure to note that he never mentioned anything about us needing liability insurance, which was important. Because getting an insurance policy to cover an event like this would have been *very* expensive.

Actual flyer for the NWF's first live event at the Anoka Armory.

So as we walked out of that building, I was glowing from ear to ear. I was telling Matt and Jason how we were going to do this, how the NWF would have its first major live event at the Anoka Armory, and how it was going to work. Jason, on the other hand, was not so convinced. At first, he thought that doing an event like that would be a huge mistake for us. He reminded me that we should be more concerned with recruiting newer kids to the show and polishing up our actual wrestling moves before attempting something big like this. I remember Jason's exact words, as he said, "Shawn, I think you might be biting off more than you can chew on this one," referring to the Anoka Armory, of course. And I listened to Jason very respectfully, but deep down, my gut instincts were telling me to do this event at the armory. And so with that, I stayed with my gut instincts and on the following day, I booked the Anoka Armory for Friday, May 9th, 1986.

Coming up with the initial $100 was nothing, as I had that much set a side in my savings account. But there was a lot to do to prepare for this armory event, and we only had about two-and-a-half months to do it. First and foremost, we needed to build a ring that would be suitable for the armory event itself, because the old ring from my garage was only 15 ft. x 15 ft. and 12 inches off the ground, and that was just not going to cut it. But, many of the parts of that old ring and a good portion of the lumber on it could be salvaged. So I came up with a new ring design that would end up being 16 ft. x 16 ft. and 24 inches off the ground. It was to be made out of wood and would need to be assembled on site. By using materials salvaged from the old ring, the new ring would end up costing us an additional $400. In addition to that, we needed to build a lighting assembly that could be raised above the ring, we needed flyers to hang up all around town, we needed program guides printed up for the event, and we needed tickets printed up so we could sell them in advance. All in all, we needed an additional $600 or so to come up with in order to do this event, but where was the money going to come from?

Well, for starters, I figured we needed to get sponsors. So using our idea of a program guide as a selling tool, we went throughout downtown Anoka and the surrounding communities and tried to sell spots within the program guide itself. Many of the businesses said no, and that surprised me. But not all of them, and we managed to sell about a half dozen spots at $50 each. We used that money to pay for printing costs of flyers and tickets and for the initial ring materials. Once we had the flyers and tickets printed, I held a meeting at Fred Moore after one of our practice sessions with all the kids. I told them our plans and what we were going to do as far as holding our first live event in front of the public. Everyone was ecstatic and full of enthusiasm. And watching their reaction, I knew we had a winning team to make this work. I explained that I needed them to put up as many flyers and sell as many advance tickets as possible, as we need to raise the money to pay for the rest of the costs we would be incurring. So with that, each of them took flyers and tickets and went to work.

Because this was our first event at the armory and I was uncertain of what kind of a draw we would have, I felt we needed something extra to help promote the event. So we advertised that we would be holding a $50 cash drawing for everyone who attends the event, just a little something extra to help sell tickets for the show. I also started to plug the event on our weekly cable show as well. This was critical, as our fan base had been tuning into our show each and every week, so plugging this event on our weekly show was absolutely necessary. So beginning in March, each week our show was promoting this upcoming event at the Anoka Armory. In fact, one week we held a special preview show, which solely focused on this upcoming event, which we were dubbing as *Superstars Spectacular '86*. Like *Wrestlemania*, this was going to be an annual event for us, so I wanted it to be extra special. So we hyped it up big time. One of the wrestlers had an uncle that was in a mentally handicapped center. And I was told that a good number of these residents were huge fans of our show. So I donated two-dozen tickets to the center for all of them to come, and we reserved a ringside section for them. I can't tell you how good doing that made me feel, and besides, they were big fans of our show.

Jason Clauson and Sgt. Smash
on Superstars Spectacular '86 preview show.

During March and April, a few new kids joined the show. Chris Hanson brought in brothers Chris and Jay Downs. Chris Downs called himself *The Ice Dragon*, and his brother went by *The Fly*. Terry Block and Chad Randall both joined up by calling the NWF Hotline, and they formed a tag team called *The Invaders*. Jerry Wellman joined the league after being recruited by his two cousins, Tim Holland and Troy Otto. Jerry became *Conan*, and formed a tag team with his cousin, Tim, as they would later dominate the NWF as *The Barbarians*. There was one kid who was causing fights and not getting along with anyone in and out of the ring, and that was Chris Eyrich. And after several warnings, he had to be suspended from the league indefinitely in the interest of the entire show. Jay Downs replaced him in the lineup for the upcoming armory event.

The wrestlers managed to sell about 60 or so tickets in advance, and between that, the sponsors, and some money my parents loaned me, the Anoka Armory event was a go. We just needed to hope we could bring in at least $250 at the gate on the night of the event to cover the rest of the armory rental fee. About a week before the event, I invited all the kids over to my house for a final meeting to go over the event itself, so that we could all be prepared for what would be expected of us on the day of the event. I had also set up our new ring in the backyard so that all the kids could get a chance to get comfortable with the new ring design by trying it out for themselves. I also wanted to let them know that because of our dedication and teamwork over the past few months, the Anoka Armory event was no longer a dream but a soon-to-be reality. I then asked them to give each other a round of applause, and they did. The last thing I told them was that next Friday night would be a night that we all would never forget, and to mark my words on that. For the next week, I was a nervous wreck. Both excited and worried, questions filled my mind. Would the event be a success or a disaster? Would there be enough ticket sales on the night of the event to cover our remaining expenses? Would the fans like us, or hate us? Would our new ring work flawlessly? What would it be like going down the isle to the ring? What would it be like wrestling in front of real fans? All these questions were just a few days away from being answered.

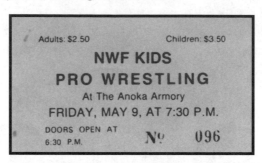

Actual ticket for the Anoka Armory event in May of 1986.

Chapter 12
Superstars Spectacular '86

I cannot put into words the anticipation I was feeling the week prior to May 9th, as it was so emotionally intense. I can remember just counting the days leading up to that night. There were a few things I had done to try to help promote this event during the past month, and one thing was I had contacted the offices of the AWA, the *American Wrestling Association.* As it turned out, their office was located in the Twin Cities and was promoted by Verne Gagne. So I introduced myself, sent a few copies of our show, and explained about our upcoming event at the Anoka Armory. Shortly afterwards, a guy by the name of Roy Nelson contacted me. He was Verne Gagne's agent. I spent some time on the phone with him and he was a really nice guy. The AWA had no problem with what we were doing, and offered to help out. They wanted to have us come on their show and do an interview to help promote our event at the armory, but due to the short notice, we did not have enough time, and that never materialized. But to be in contact with one of the three major wrestling promotions and to be acknowledged by them, that was extremely gratifying to me. I stayed in contact with Roy Nelson for most of that summer, and we even mentioned his name as "AWA Agent" on the ending credits of our cable show each week, the AWA knew we were doing it, and never objected. Also, I phoned in our event to the *Minneapolis Star Tribune* Sports Department to see if we could get listed in the paper for local area sporting events, and it worked. Nothing can beat a little free advertising.

Minneapolis Star Tribune listing in
the sports section, May 1986.

The day of Friday, May 9th, 1986, had finally arrived, and we were all very excited, yet nervous as well. We got to the Anoka Armory at about 2 p.m., and we began to set up. First we had to assemble the ring. Then we had to erect the lighting unit above the ring. All the folding chairs had to be set up in four sections surrounding the ring. We had to set up the ticket booth at the front door. We had to set up the camera unit that was going to tape the event. We also had to set up the commentary station for play-by-play, and the PA system for the ring announcer and wrestler introduction music. We had to do all this in about four hours time, but I had the entire crew of kids in our league helping, so it went fairly quick. For that first event, I did not have the time or the money to cover buying any concessions, so I had let the Blaine Johnsville Lions Club handle all of our concessions that night. Later, I learned how much of a moneymaker that was and wished we would have done it ourselves.

All that day, I in particular, was a nervous wreck. My main concern was ticket sales. Going into that event, we only had about

60 advance tickets sold, and I was concerned about being able to have enough people show up that night at the door in order to cover our costs. Besides the $250 for the armory we owed, I had borrowed another $200 or so in addition to that. So we needed at least an additional 100 paid spectators to come through the gate that night. During the set-up, I had wired a live feed from our stationary camera that was filming the event out in the armory into the locker room, so we could monitor what was happening out on the floor as well as know when we were being introduced for each match. The doors opened at 6:30 p.m., and the people began to fill into the armory.

The Super Ds in the ring during the NWFs first public card in 1986.

I don't remember what I was doing, but just prior to show time, I remember my dad coming into the locker room and saying, "So are you ready to do this, you guys have a couple hundred people out there." My eyes nearly popped out of my head as I turned to the nearby monitor and looked into the screen to see hundreds of fans seated around the ring, and they were still coming in. I remember the locker room getting silent as we all stared into the monitor in awe of the large crowd on hand. At that point, we were all getting nervous, not for the gate sales as I was previously worried about, but for the fact that we were about to perform in front of *hundreds* of paid spectators for the first time.

At 7:30 p.m., we began our first match. Jason Clauson was our ring announcer and he introduced both *The Black Panther* and *The Tokyo Terror*. *The Black Panther* was a new character being played by Steve Owens where he wore a black ninja suit. Even though *The Tokyo Terror* was supposed to be a bad guy, and *The Black Panther* a good guy, they both were applauded as they were introduced. I guess the fans at first were not sure if it was appropriate or not to "boo" any of us kids. As the bell was rung, someone mentioned that we did not have a referee in the ring, and so I quickly told Chad Rancour to throw on a referee shirt and go out there to ref the match. It was a shaky start, but the match went well, and it went to a time limit draw. It was not the most exciting match, but I knew that the next one was going to be.

Following that match, the next one was for the Lightweight Tag Team titles, and it had *The Super Ds* defending against *The Rough Russians*. The only problem was that one of *The Rough Russians* could not make it, so we had to get a replacement. So we substituted one of the *Rough Russians* with their new manager, *The Iranian Sheik*. This was a brand new character we had just recently brought into the league. He was a little bit too big to be a lightweight, but that just added to the drama of the match itself. I had Jason introduce this and announce that *The Iranian Sheik* was substituting for one of the Russians. Any doubt from the fans regarding if they should "boo" any of us kids or not was quickly gone because as Jason introduced the Russian and Sheik team, they got "booed" from just about everyone in the building. This was one of the best matches of the night, full of great moves, and huge fan reaction. It ended in great controversy too, as we had the Russian team win the titles from *The Super Ds*.

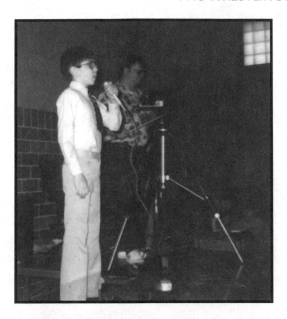

*CJ Pregler doing the play by play during
the Anoka Armory event.*

The remaining matches all went well, *The Ring Warriors* defeated *The Eliminators*, *The Invaders* defeated *The US Enforcers*, where *Slick Steenerson* actually dressed up as a woman when he entered the ring. *Sgt. Samsh, Rough Ryan*, and *Kid USA Kelsey* defeated *The Russian Destroyers* and *Bull Dog Butcher* for the 6-Man titles. In the end of this match, The Sheik and the Russians turned on their partner *Bull Dog Butcher* for losing the 6-Man Championship. In the World Tag Team title bout, *The Barbarians* defended against *Mr. X and Mr. X II*. Going into this match, *The Xs* were the good guys, and *The Barbarians* were the bad guys. But the crowd was cheering for *The Barbarians*, so "go figure," I guess. But during this match, our first major problem occurred as the right corner of the ring mat ended up breaking. Our ring was made out of wood, and it had no spring to absorb the falls of all the kids getting slammed and whatnot. And so during this match, that one section snapped and for the rest of the night, we all had to avoid that particular corner of the mat. You could not tell by looking at it, but it would sag down when you walked over that corner of the ring.

Finally, it was my turn, and my opponent *Pretty Boy Taylor* was already out in the ring, and then I was introduced. I remember Jason introduced me as I was walking down to the ring, and I cannot tell you how it felt to have hundreds of fans cheering for me as I made my way to the ring—there was (and is) nothing else like it. We had a decent match, and in the end, we were both counted out. As I started to leave the ring at the end of my match, I was surrounded by a bunch of younger kids; there must have been a dozen of them. And they all had pens in hand and wanted my autograph for their program guides. I can't describe how good one feels when you have a bunch of kids, aged 7 and up, all looking up to you as a role model. To them, you are their *hero*. When you can touch a kid's life like that, nothing else compares. It is absolutely priceless.

The $50 cash drawing ended up getting won by one of the mentally handicap residents that we had given free tickets to, and needless to say, he got the biggest round of applause that night. But due to the ring breaking, we were unable to have our scheduled battle royal as the main event. So we had a special "Lumberjack Match" in its place where all the wrestlers would surround the ring. The match had *The Iranian Sheik* against *Bull Dog Butcher* feeding off their recent parting earlier on in their 6-Man tag match. It went over well, and the fans did not seem to mind about the switch.

Actual program guide for Superstars Spectacular '86.

All in all, it was a very successful night. We went out and did something that had never been done before, and we did it very well. We had between 300 and 350 fans in attendance, and we sold several of our program guides, bringing in enough money to cover the remaining costs and leave us with around $800 to spare. And as the fans left the building that night, all of us in the league were on proverbial cloud nine. I remember several kids from our show coming up to me and asking, "So, Shawn, where are we going next on tour?" They were all full of emotion and so was I. How could you not be? At that moment, we felt like we could successfully perform in a new town every night. But as I look back at it now, that entire armory event was a *real* gamble. This one event would determine the fate of our league. If it were successful, we would grow from it. But if it failed, it could have been the end of the entire league. And it could have gone either way that night. But as luck would have it for us, it was a complete success, both publicly and emotionally. And so with that, later that night as we finished cleaning up, I booked the armory for July 26th, where the NWF would once again return to the Anoka Armory.

Chapter 13
Summertime Blues

That night after our first big public card, I thought I would call in our match results into the *Minneapolis Star Tribune*. Back in those days, after a professional wrestling card, they had always printed the results in the paper in the sports section the following day. And sure enough, the following morning our results were printed in the paper. I have to admit that the media was truly treating us as equals in this wrestling business we were doing. That following morning, we had a taping to do at Fred Moore Jr. High for our weekly show, and even though it was bad scheduling on my part, I figured that hardly anyone would show up due to the fact that we had just done that big card at the armory the night before. But that following morning, just about every kid showed up, all buzzing over the armory from the night before.

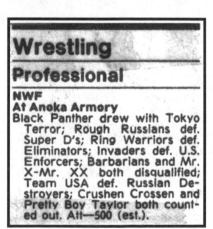

Match results printed in the Minneapolis Star Tribune, May 1986.

Because of the success of the first armory card, we had a lot of new kids who joined shortly after it. Chris Barger and Mike Bauer had each attended our armory event and asked if they could join. They were 17-year olds, and being 16 myself, I had no objections. They would become a tag team known as *The Rack -n-Roll Express*. As it would turn out, both Mike and Chris would become pretty helpful behind the scenes as well, as they wanted to help improve the show. David Dixon also joined after attending the armory event, calling himself *Dixie Dave*. Mike Whaley and Nick Dumas also came in as a tag team calling themselves *The Mr. Nice Guys* (*Mr. Macho* and *Mr. Destroyer*, respectfully). On the next few shows we taped, we started to promote our next event at the Anoka Armory just as we did before.

Even though our first armory card was a success, our wrestling ring we used for it was not. And having sections snap during major events was something I did not want to have repeated. And for this, I discussed the situation with Steve. We both agreed that we needed to do something different with our ring design. And as luck would have it, I received a phone call from a guy out in Hutchinson, MN. As it turned out, he owned an actual professional wrestling ring that he was no longer using and wanted to know if we would be interested in buying it. So Steve and I drove out there to take a look at it. The ring was 20 ft. x 20 ft. and 24 inches off the ground. But unlike our old ring, this one was made of steel and had a center spring in the middle of it. And best of all, the guy only wanted $500 plus our old ring that we were using in trade. *This was a steal*, we thought. We agreed to the offer and made plans to pick it up the following week.

On the day we were supposed to go out and pick up the ring, Steve called me and told me he could not drive out there with me to get the ring, I forget the reason why. I didn't have a driver's license yet, so I was relying on Steve to be able to do this. I was extremely mad at Steve for pulling this on me with such short notice. So I called Mike Bauer to see if he could help since I knew he could drive. He was not happy either as he had plans that evening, but he changed them and offered to bail me out. We used his family station wagon and a large open trailer to go out and pick up the ring. When we arrived, we had to actually take the ring apart as the seller did not have it disassembled. This only added to Mike's frustration. Once we had it loaded up and were driving down the highway heading back home, I remember hearing this screeching noise coming from behind us. Also, I could feel the whole station wagon slightly rocking from side to side as well. So I looked back, and the trailer with our ring was fish tailing from side to side so bad that the tires were smoking and it was nearly sliding into oncoming traffic. Mike had noticed it at the same time, and all I remember him saying as he gripped the steering wheel as tight as he could trying to maintain control was, "*Fudge!*" only he said the real thing. He was extremely ticked off. Because of the severity of the trailer fish tailing, I was concerned we were going to end up flipping over. So I told Mike we should pull over and see what we could do. We took most of the heavy parts of steel out of the trailer and put them into the back of the station wagon to balance out the load, and that did the trick. It's funny looking back at it now, but at the time, it was a pretty scary thing.

Mike Bauer from May of 1986.

With about a month to go prior to the next armory event, our old nemesis Scott Tronson once again pulled a fast one on us. After watching some of our recent shows, he decided to suspend us for one month from Group W Studios. In addition, he also had our weekly show suspended from being aired as well. The reason you ask? He claimed we were advertising on public access. *Advertising?* I thought. You see, one of the rules about having programs air on public access is that you cannot advertise products or services for the purpose of making a profit. And according to Scott, by us advertising our upcoming armory events, we were violating that rule. I was absolutely livid with Scott. I told him that what we were doing was *promoting* ourselves, and that was not advertising at all. But Scott did not agree and stood his ground. This was disastrous for the league. Without our weekly show being aired, no one would know about our upcoming armory event. Our weekly show was the only way we were promoting the upcoming event, as I did not even do up posters for this second card.

While we were suspended, my good friend and league cofounder Charley Lane came up for a visit during the month of June. He was both impressed and proud of all I had done with the wrestling show we started nearly two years ago. In fact, I had him scheduled to appear on the next big armory card in July, it was going to be "The Return of Luxury Lane." However, I got in trouble with my mom over something or another, and she said that Charley would have to leave for back home earlier as punishment. So Charley had to go back earlier than he planned on, and he would not be able to make the upcoming armory card. I could not have been more disappointed as I really wanted Charley to be able to do an armory event with us and experience it for himself. I was both mad at my mom and mad at myself for letting that happen in the first place.

And to make matters worse, Mr. Daniels calls me from Fred Moore Jr. High and tells me that our six-month pilot was up, and that the he had decided against letting us permanently use the Golden Gloves Boxing ring. His reason was because the school had one of the kid's parents call up and complain about our show and the way I was running it. This was Chris Eyrich's mom, the kid who we suspended from the league due to him causing problems both in and out of the ring. After pleading with Mr. Daniels and getting nowhere, I called up Mr. Stewart at the school district headquarters to see if he could help us. And unlike before, he did not have any advice for us. He went on to say that we basically blew it. I could not understand why neither one of them would listen to nor believe my side of the story, and I always wondered if Scott Tronson had something to do with this as well? I guess I would never know for sure. So after getting a new wrestling ring to improve our league, we took two critical blows that nearly killed our show all together. But I was not about go down that easily.

The first thing I needed to address was our weekly cable show. We needed to get back on the air, and more importantly, we needed to be able to promote our upcoming armory events on the show itself. So I went downtown to the Anoka City Hall, and I met with city cable commissioner Terry O'Connell. He had the power and authority over all of the cable operations in our community, including all of public access. I explained to Mr. O'Connell what had happened regarding our suspension by Scott Tronson, and the reasons why. Then I explained our view on it, in that we were nonprofit, and that we're only *promoting* ourselves. I remember the look on Mr. O'Connell's face, and I could tell that he was very disappointed in this development. He told me that he was going to make some calls, and he would get back to me later that afternoon. After a few hours, I got the call from Terry, and he said that our suspension was to be lifted immediately and that we would be able to promote our upcoming events on the show as we were doing before. The only stipulation was that now we can no longer mention ticket prices on the air. I thanked Terry several times over the phone, as I was so excited. As it turned out, Terry was a *huge* fan of our show, and so having him on our side really helped out in situations like this.

As far as losing Fred Moore goes, it was probably a good thing. The ring we were using there had no give to it whatsoever, as it was basically a boxing ring. And during our final taping at Fred Moore, I had a match against *The Tokyo Terror* where during the match I gave him a forward pile driver. During that maneuver, his head slipped completely out from my legs. The end result was Peter landing completely on top of his head with all of my weight pulling him down. He was like a human pogo stick. It was a real scary moment, as Peter did not get up right away. As it turned out, it was only a stinger and he would be fine. But it was a real close call. That was the only time I had ever done anything negligent in the ring that put another person at risk. Yet, I felt terrible. Peter had to quit the show after that, because his parent's thought that incident was just too close of a call. The NWF lost a great character with *The Tokyo Terror*. Peter was a great athlete and performer, and a good friend. A day does not go by that I still do not think of that moment, and how lucky we all were that he didn't get paralyzed from that incident.

Peter Nguyen aka "The Tokyo Terror" from 1986.

I remember finally going back into Group W Cable since our suspension had been lifted. And Scott Tronson was not happy with us by any means. He just gave us the old cold shoulder treatment. I asked him, "So we can use the equipment again, right, Scott?" And he replied, "Yes, Shawn, you can. Mr. O'Connell is our boss and what he says goes. But we still feel you did wrong, so don't expect anyone to treat you very kindly around here." He was really speaking for himself, as everyone else treated me fine except him.

The only problem with all of this was our normal weekly timeslot was temporarily filled with other programs due to the suspension, so our show was still another two weeks out from being aired, which would put us back on the air just one week prior to the next big event at the armory on July 26th. That was hardly enough time to get the word out for this next big card we were about to do. All in all, we had been off the air for over a month, and this was not good from a promoting standpoint at all. I really wished we would have printed posters to put up around town, but I was so busy in getting our new ring, dealing with the Fred Moore situation, and getting the suspension lifted, that I never had the time to get posters printed up. So with less than a week to go, we were about to do the next armory card, and I was once again a nervous wreck, and this time, I had good reason to be.

Chapter 14
Lessons Learned

Roughly a week prior to the armory event, Tom Yelle, the local sports reporter for *ABC Newspapers* contacted me for an interview. He wanted to write a story about our league for the paper. *ABC Newspapers* covered most of the northern suburbs of the Twin Cities. So we did the interview and on July 18th, it came out in the paper. It was a feature story on the front page of the sports section, and it went on to a full page mock-up within the paper. It was very well done and gave us some great publicity. During the interview, I really pushed him on how Fred Moore shafted us out from using the boxing ring a few weeks back in hopes that we could get some decent press coverage on that whole ordeal, but he chose not to go into that in the write-up he did, which I guess I couldn't blame him.

Full page write-up in ABC Newspapers in July of 1986.

So we finally arrive to Saturday, July 26th, 1986, for our big return to the Anoka Armory. We decided to do the second card on Saturday rather than Friday this time because someone mentioned it would be a better night to attract fans. Going into the event, I was very concerned about the ticket sales. We only had about 30 advance tickets sold, and we were just hours away from show time. I remember being in the locker room and just pacing back and forth talking to different kids about the whole situation. They all knew I was concerned. Once the doors opened, I remember I kept looking out the windows of the dressing room to see how many people were coming into the armory, and it wasn't many. But I kept thinking to myself that fans would show up like they did last time and it would be fine, or so I hoped.

On the card that night, we had *The Invaders* scheduled against *The Ice Dragon* and *The Fly*, and we learned about an hour before show time that Chad Randall's (*Invader II*) grandmother had passed away, so he was not going to make it. So we had Mike Bauer fill in during this match for Chad. Steve had this huge friend of his named Larry Rhode along with him. I mean this guy was big. He worked out daily in the gym and you could tell. He wanted to know if we needed any help, so I asked him to run the camera that night, and he did just that. But Steve had other ideas up his sleeve as to what he wanted to do with his friend, which we will get into a little bit later.

Once we arrived at bell time, we had a whopping 50 people in the entire audience. The place was *dead*. At the time, I was completely baffled by this. *Why did they not come like they did back in May?* I thought to myself. And for the rest of the night, I kept thinking of what we could have possibly done wrong in preparing for this event. It's one thing when you have a decent crowd to go out to and wrestle, but it's embarrassing when you have to go out to a near-empty armory and do the same thing. I remember I heard a few kids complaining about the situation at hand with the small crowd, and I then reminded them that those 50 or so fans out there paid to see us put on a wrestling card, and that's exactly what we are going to do. I don't care how many people are out there, whether it's 5 fans or 500 fans, we put on the same show regardless. They both nodded in agreement. But I certainly understood their point, and deep down I was feeling it too.

*The Super Ds in tag team action from
the July armory card in 1986.*

I remember when it came time for my match that night; I was working against Steve's *Mr. X* character for the title. As I started to make my way to the dressing room door to go out to the ring, all the kids lined up in a path to the door as they all gave me some skin as I made my way to the door, and thanked me for bringing them this far. They must have all planned it out ahead of time, and it was kind of emotional for me to see my friends and colleagues all come together to show me respect like that. That is the way we worked in the locker room back then, we were all like one big family back there. They all knew I was concerned about the attendance that night, and doing what they did just prior to me going out for my match made me forget all about it. Steve and I ended up doing a 30-minute time limit draw, and we gave them everything we had, it was one of the hardest matches I ever worked. I remember afterwards, I went out to the concession stand and grabbed a few sodas to quench my thirst and some older fan in his mid-30s came up to me and wanted to shake my hand. He then told me that was one of the best matches he had ever seen. I thanked him for the compliment and walked back into the dressing room thinking to myself, *Hey at least that guy got his money's worth.*

LESSONS LEARNED

After we cleaned up and left the armory, we had maybe $400 to spare after paying all the costs for the armory event itself. That night when I got home, I was completely confused about what went wrong that night as far as the attendance was concerned. Why did we not have the 300 plus fans like we did the last time out? What did we do wrong? Yet, I could not find the answers to those questions. So later that night after reviewing the tape of the armory card we had just done, I took a walk down to the store. It was a clear night, and the warm summer night's breeze was blowing slightly, and as I walked slowly down the street, it all started to make sense to me. I started to compare the first armory card with the one we just did as far as what we did to prepare for both of them. For the first event, we promoted it for two months every week on our weekly cable show, but for this last card, we were off the air for a month and only got back on the air with a week to go. During the first armory event, I had all the kids in the show selling tickets to friends and neighbors, but for this last one, I did not do that at all. In the first armory event, we made up posters and hung them up all over town, and for this last card, we did not print up a single flyer. And that night, I came to realize that I had just learned a valuable lesson in the game of life. In order to be successful with an event of this magnitude, you need to promote and advertise it like there is no tomorrow. It was those things we did the first time that made it work, and it was those same things we lacked on in the second event that made it fail. And I said to myself as I walked home from the store that night, we are going back to that armory once again. And this time, it will be a *complete sellout*.

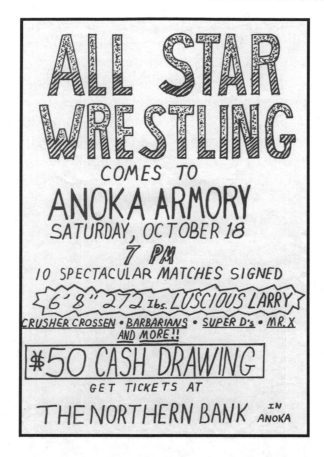

Actual flyer for the Anoka Armory card in October of 1986.

So for the next event, I decided to book the armory for October 18th, which was about 2 1/2 months away. This way, we would have plenty of time to promote it each week on our regular show. Steve then asked me what I thought about having him go against his friend, Larry, for the main event that night, sort of a special attraction. At first I was not sure about it, after all we were supposed to be kids pro wrestling. And this guy was a monster, nearly 250 pounds of solid muscle. But Steve said he would train him personally, and they would work out a really good match. And because I was always looking for unique ways to attract fans, *what would be better than this?* I thought. Larry wanted to call himself *Luscious Larry,* so I figured we could build up this Luscious Larry character as the next "big thing." So I agreed to it, and we started to hype him up big time. Every week we kept showing his picture and announced that as an extra-added attraction, this 6-ft.-6-inch, 265-pound Olympian, *Luscious Larry*, would be facing the NWF's very own *Pretty Boy Taylor* for the main event on our upcoming Anoka Armory card. We basically made Larry out to be an outsider, as if he was a real professional wrestler coming into our league to take on our top heel, which at that time was Steve's *Pretty Boy Taylor* character. I did not let Larry wrestle on the show at all leading up to the armory card. My idea was that we needed to keep him completely mysterious to the fans so that they would buy a ticket to the upcoming event in order to see *Luscious Larry's* debut.

Larry Rhode aka "Luscious Larry" from the summer of 1986.

I then made up posters for the event and printed up tickets. We got several sponsors for the event, including most of the banks and a few car dealerships. Around this time, I asked both Mike Bauer and Chris Barger to join the NWF *producers council.* They were both helping out big time and were more than team players, so I really wanted them on the NWF team. They both accepted the offer without hesitation. During the summer, Chris Barger had started to play double duty on the show. Not only was he Mike's tag team partner, but he also served as the NWF's new interviewer and match commentator. Chris was really good at it too. During matches, he and *Bull Dog Butcher* started doing color commentary together, and they made a great team together on the microphones, where *Butcher* served as the "heel" commentator.

In order to tape new weekly shows for our cable TV timeslots, I would sneak and set up our wrestling ring in my backyard during the day while my mom was at work, and all the guys would come over and we would tape our matches for our cable show, then we would disassemble the ring before my mom would get home. We did this throughout the summer, and it worked out fine. But wintertime was just around the corner, and we would need to come up with a solution that would give us a normal place to do weekly shows from, but for now we just used my backyard.

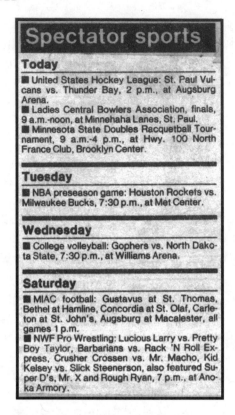

*Minneapolis Star Tribune listing in the
sports section, October 1986.*

About a month before the armory card, we had to suspend Chris Downs for problems that were going on in and out of the ring. Chris was a great heel character on our show, but sometimes he would take his act behind the scenes, and it would wind up hurting him in the end. But that suspension was decided on from the NWF *producers council*, as I always got along with Chris myself, but it would not be right for me to overstep their decision. It was only a temporary suspension, so he would be able to return soon.

Around the beginning of August, Steve and myself attended a local PWA (*Pro Wrestling America*) card that was promoted by Eddie Sharkey. The PWA was the only other minor league in town at the time, and Steve and I decided to go to one of their shows. Afterwards, we introduced ourselves to Eddie in the back dressing room. Eddie was very open and outgoing with us, and he was aware of what we were doing. He thought that what we had going with our kids pro wrestling show was very cool and perhaps we could work together sometime and put a show on together. Steve and I were just thrilled that Eddie actually acknowledged us much less offering to work together with us on a possible event. This would be the start of a lasting relationship that we would have with Eddie Sharkey for the next several years.

As we were coming closer and closer to the October 18th armory event, my main goal was to sell out this event. So every week, we kept pushing the interview segments on our weekly show to help promote the upcoming event, and we kept hyping Luscious Larry as a special added attraction. I had all the kids selling tickets in advance just as before on the first event, and we plastered the town with posters everywhere we could. In addition, I also rented a lighted sign to place out front of the armory for a few weeks prior to the event. Also, I set up a deal with 107.9 FM, the local radio station in town. We would give them around a couple dozen free tickets to give away during their morning show, where in turn, our event would get a free plug during the process. This is another way to get free publicity. In fact, a couple weeks prior to the 18th, Larry, Steve, and myself all stopped in at the station to drop off the free tickets, and they asked us if we would like to go live on the air for a promotional plug for the upcoming event. How could we say no to that? We were on for about 5-10 minutes, and we had a lot of fun with it.

With two weeks to go, I received a call from the Northern Bank in downtown Anoka. They said they had sold all their tickets and were requesting more. I had given them 100 tickets to start with, and I was shocked to know that they were all sold. I gave them an additional 75 tickets. And then a week later, they called again requesting more tickets. By the time we got to the day of the event, we had nearly 250 advance tickets sold. *Perhaps my wish for a sellout just may become a reality after all*, I thought.

```
┌─────────────────────────────────────┐
│           N⁰   110                   │
│     NWF All Star Wrestling           │
│        At The Anoka Armory           │
│                                      │
│           SATURDAY                   │
│     OCTOBER 18, 7:00 p.m.            │
│                                      │
│     ADMIT ONE ADULT: $4.50          │
└─────────────────────────────────────┘
```

Actual ticket from the Anoka Armory event, October 1986.

Chapter 15
How Sweet It Is

By the time we reached the date of October 18th, the excitement in the air was thick and contagious. Based on the advance ticket sales, I borrowed some extra money from my mom to help pay for extra concessions as I knew we were going to have a big crowd on hand, and I did not want to run out of any food or beverages. As the doors opened, we had a huge crowd waiting to come in. And they kept coming, one after another. The next thing we knew, we had sold nearly 200 tickets at the door and nearly 450 people overall in attendance. Roughly 15 minutes prior to show time, my dad came back to tell us we had just sold out the Anoka Armory. The whole locker room erupted in an enormous cheer, as this was our goal all along. Several of the kids came up to me congratulating me at that moment, and I couldn't have been happier.

Actual program guide for the October armory card.

Then a few minutes later, one of the volunteers running the ticket counter came into the locker room and said there was a fan upset about our event. Apparently, he thought that this event was going to be a regular professional wrestling card from the AWA, and he felt that our posters were misleading. You see, we had advertised the event as "All Star Wrestling" this time rather than "Kids Pro Wrestling" as we had done in the past. So I went out to address the situation. I told the guy that if he was *that* upset, he could just have his money back and leave if he liked. But in the end, he said he would just stay for the event.

Jason Clauson was our ring announcer for the night, and word of this incident with that one fan soon got to him, and just before show time, Jason came up to me all concerned about it. Jason felt that perhaps the reason we had so many people at the armory was because they really did think it was going to be *real* professional wrestling. Jason said he was afraid to go out there because when he announces the first match and they realize that it is in fact kids pro wrestling, he would get "booed" out of the arena and fans would start throwing things at him. I remember telling him, "Calm down, Jason, it was just one fan who felt that way. The rest of those people out there know what to expect here tonight, trust me." I then told him to go out there and just introduce the event by welcoming everyone to "NWF, Junior Professional Wrestling." And then you will know right away how they feel, and I assured him they would give him a warm applause.

The NWF's first ever sellout from the Anoka Armory
in October of 1986.

So with that, an extremely nervous Jason Clauson went out to the largest crowd we had ever faced and did just what I told him to do. He announced, "Welcome to the NWF, Junior Professional Wrestling," and with that the entire armory burst into a *huge* applause. I would never forget that moment, as this was probably the greatest moment in our league's entire history. I remember watching the monitor in the dressing room and seeing the fans reaction to that introduction by Jason, and I had never felt more proud of what we had accomplished with the league up to that point in time.

Back on the July armory card, we started using normal older referees for the matches, instead of us kids. Normally, these guys were just older friends of the kids in the show who volunteered to do it. One of these guys was Rick Pitts. The only problem was he was an alcoholic and half the time he would show up to the armory all drunk. And needless to say, it would affect his performance. This happened at the July card really bad, and so I told Rick that he cannot show up drunk like that ever again, or he would not be allowed to ref any of the matches. Fortunately, he showed up sober on the October 18th card. Besides his drinking habits, Rick was a really nice guy. And when he was sober, he did a great refereeing job in the ring.

During the card, one of the kids in the locker room came up to me and said some Mike kid was outside the door and asked to see me. *Mike?* I thought. I went to the door, and there stood non other than *Merciless Mike Ackermann* in person. It was a total shocker to see Mike at the event. He just wanted to stop by and say hello and wish us luck on the card. We talked for a bit about the old days and shared a few memories, but because I was busy with the event going on, I could not spend much time with him. But it meant so much to me to see Mike there at the armory supporting what he himself was once a part of. Mike was always a class act in my book, and him knocking on the door to see me that night just proved that point all the more.

*Rattlesnake Jake has a figure four leg lock
on Invader II from the armory.*

For this event, Larry wanted to make a grand entrance into the armory that would really stand out. So instead of coming into the armory from the locker rooms like the rest of us, he was planning on making his entrance from the garage area of the armory by having the big door open up, where he would have a bunch of smoke created from dry ice come rolling out as he walks out from it. It was a great concept. So hearing the news, Troy Steenerson (*Slick Steenerson*) decides he wants to do something similar for his entrance too, so he grabs the fire extinguisher hanging on the wall and asks me if I could just blow it off behind him as he walks out. I figured, OK, no big deal. Well, as it turned out, it was one of those powdered filled extinguishers rather than a CO_2 extinguisher as we both had originally thought. So as Troy walked out for his match and I did the extinguisher behind him, white powder goes all over the place creating a huge cloud of powder filled smoke. This stuff got all over the place, and as you watched the tape of the event, you could see this hazy cloud floating into the camera's view that would eventually fill the entire armory, it was a real mess. And if you were close by it, it was hard to breath. Needless to say, it was a bad idea and it made a real mess to clean up afterwards.

All the matches that night went over pretty well. In addition to our cast of regulars, we had a few new faces that joined the league along with a guy who made a return from a long absence. Terry Kosnapal made his debut and showed some real talent for his first time out in a tag match against Chris Hanson (*Sgt. Smash*) and Ryan Kelsey (*Rough Ryan*). Brian Peterson made his return after being absent for nearly a year. It was great to see Brian again, and we used to him to fill in for Chris Barger of *The Rack-n-Roll Express*, who could not make it that night. One of our main matches that evening involved a new lightweight tag team that joined back in August calling themselves *The Blade Runners*. They were a pair of brothers named Todd and Troy Sufka, and they were supposed to wrestle Todd and Troy Dusosky, known in the ring as *The Super Ds*. But about a week prior to the card, the Dusosky brothers' mom decided she did not want her kids wrestling on this event due to their soccer tournament they were involved in that same weekend. She was afraid that they might have gotten hurt, I guess. But she did allow them to come to the event. So we had them go out to the ring and get stripped of their titles and awarded them to *The Blade Runners*, as I felt that would help build up a possible rematch for a future date.

Little league action from the October Anoka Armory card in 1986.

When we got to Larry's match, his grand entrance went over like a charm. It was a real eye-catcher, I must say, and I remember Jason saying afterwards that he had to bite his bottom lip as he announced Larry to the ring while he watched this entrance of his. The match was well planned out and full of great moves. It went over very well. In the end, Steve (*Pretty Boy Taylor*) won the match by using a fluke pin on Larry that was highly controversial. This way, it would help lead to a rematch at the next event.

All in all, October 18th, 1986, was a huge success for our league. We had cleared nearly $2,000 from that event, and it was our largest crowd ever at the Anoka Armory, as it was a complete sellout with more than 450 people in attendance. A few weeks later, as a special thanks to all the kids in the show, we held a pizza party at Dell's Pizza in downtown Anoka. We had reserved the lower basement area of Dell's where we held the party along with a private screening of the October armory card. It was a lot of fun, and we had a blast that night.

At the end of October, I decided to take a break from the Anoka Armory and venture off to another nearby city, Brooklyn Park. I went ahead and booked the Brooklyn Park Armory for December 19th, and we started promoting it on our weekly cable show. Also, I set up a special card at Sandburg Middle School for a community event that took place after school. Mrs. Kiphuth was in charge of the community school program at Sandburg, and she was my 6th grade teacher back in the day. So setting this up was a piece of cake. Besides, it worked great for us as far as having a place to tape a few new shows for our regular weekly cable show. About 70 some kids showed up to watch, as we had the ring set up in the back gym. The entire event went over quite well, other than one of The Super D brothers taking the bus home by mistake and missing the entire thing.

PROFESSIONAL WRESTLING SPECTACULAR

LIVE

AT THE CHAMPLIN AMERICAN LEGION
SUNDAY, NOV. 30,1986
6:00 P.M.

APPEARING:

NORTHEAST WRECKING CREW
DIVISION OF BAD COMPANY

| WOMENS MATCH | THE TERMINATORS |
| DERRICK DUKES | HIGH ROLLERS |

NATIONAL WRESTLING FEDERATION

CRUSHER CROSSEN	LUSCIOUS LARRY
VS	VS
MR. X	PRETTY BOY TAYLOR

TICKETS AVAILABLE AT:
FIRST NATIONAL BANKS IN ANOKA & CHAMPLIN
$7.00 IN ADVANCE - $8.00 AT THE DOOR

*Actual flyer for the NWF/PWA dual promotional event
from November of 1986.*

In November of 1986, Eddie Sharkey asked me if I would be interested in doing a joint promotional event with him at the Champlin Legion. What he wanted from our league were two matches with our best guys and to help promote the event on our weekly cable show. I agreed immediately and decided to use Larry, Steve, and myself where Steve would play double duty as being both *Pretty Boy Taylor* and *Mr. X* in the mask. So our two matches were *Crusher Crossen* vs. *Mr. X* and *Luscious Larry* vs. *Pretty Boy Taylor*. I chose to use us three because I knew we were the best guys from our league, and I did not want to let Eddie down thinking that maybe we could do more of these if it went over well. I used our production crew to tape the entire event, and the footage was used on our weekly show. It's interesting to note that back on November 30th, 1986, this was the first-ever, dual-promotional event that ever took place in the Twin Cities area by two different wrestling leagues. The card went over well, and the place was packed with close to 300 people in attendance. The fans really got into our two matches that night, and that made me feel good. Eddie was happy with us as well, and this made me feel even better. In my match that night, I dropped the title to Steve's *Mr. X* character, as we were planning on me winning it back on our upcoming Brooklyn Park Armory card in roughly three weeks time on December 19th.

With less than a month to go, we started to hang up posters throughout the Brooklyn Park area for our upcoming event. As for selling advance tickets, I set up an account at Dayton's Ticket Outlet, as this was the main outlet that was used at the time for selling tickets for any event in the Twin Cities metro area. As we were coming to a close in 1986, this was a huge year for our league. We went from the basement of Fred Moore at the start of the year to promoting four major armory events as well as doing a dual promotional event with Eddie Sharkey's PWA promotion, just to name a few endeavors. We had accomplished so much during the year, that we felt that we were literally unstoppable. Nothing was going to get in our way on the road to success, or so it seemed.

New champion reigns in NWF

There is a new world champion presently reigning in the National Wrestling Federation--NWF. He is Mr. X.

Mr. X upset the previous NWF champion, Crusher Crossen, by gaining a controversial fall Nov. 30 during a special wrestling card at the Champlin American Legion. The new champion, however, will have to defend that title Dec. 19 at the Brooklyn Park Armory against former champion. Tickets are now on sale at Dayton's outlets.

Other winners on the Nov. 30 card co-sponsored by the NWF and PWA (Pro Wrestling America) were: Luscious Larry, Rick Rice, and the Northeast Wrecking Crew along with Rick Rice in a three-man tag-team match.

ABC Newspaper clipping on results from NWF title change from 1986.

Chapter 16
A League Divided

Towards the end of 1986, our wrestling show was at the peak of its success, and I was finding that I had less and less free time for anything else. Not that this bothered me, but every minute of my time was devoted to our wrestling show. Not only was I busy setting up the different armory cards and other events that we did such as the dual card with the PWA, I also had to maintain our weekly cable TV show which was still being syndicated around the Twin Cities and the rest of the country each and every week. And starting back on the October armory card, I was using three separate video cameras to film our major events. This meant I had one stationary camera and two remote cameras around the ringside area. Then I would take the three different sources and edit them all together so the end result would look like we had a superior multi-camera shot for the event. It looked very professional, but it took hours of editing time over several days to accomplish this just for one night's event. But I must admit, after watching the final edited product, it was always well worth it. Once I had these separate sources edited together, I would just discard and reuse all the original tapes, something I would really regret doing years later.

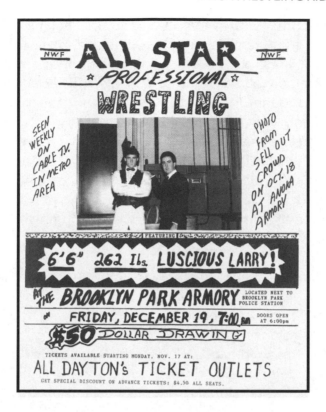

Actual Flyer for the Brooklyn Park Armory card in December 1986.

So as we approached December 19th, 1986, our advance ticket sales for Brooklyn Park were not doing very well at all, where we maybe had a dozen sold, if that. This was mostly due to Dayton's Ticket Outlet not distributing our tickets to all locations as they were contracted to do. So in most locations, if someone wanted to buy a ticket, the ticket outlet did not have the tickets on hand to sell to them. Not only did I get a complete refund from Dayton's Ticket Outlet, it was also the last time I ever used them for selling our advance tickets, as I was not impressed by their performance at all.

As we got to Brooklyn Park and began setting up, we were all working to get things ready, and I noticed Larry Rhode getting very impatient and yelling at most of us kids that were working. He was getting real bossy with everyone. So I approached him and asked him what his problem was, and he pointed at me and told me to just watch it, as he is not taking any crap from me or anyone else. At that point, my blood began to boil. *Who the hell does this guy think he is?* I thought. Steve had witnessed this whole confrontation between Larry and myself, and he came over to me trying to calm me down before I said anything back. As Steve was doing this, I asked him, "What in the hell is his problem, Steve, and whose show does he think this is?" Steve replied, "I know, I know. He is just nervous and wants everything to go smoothly, that's all. Just let it go." I started to calm down, but the whole thing really bothered me to put it mildly.

Going into that event, Larry was supposed to wrestle Steve's *Pretty Boy Taylor* character to continue their rivalry. However, Larry took it upon himself to get one of his weight-lifting buddies from the gym to go against him instead. He was calling this guy *The Warrior*. He was another big huge guy built like a brick wall. *Who is Larry to just arbitrarily change the card like that?* I thought. Again, this just added to my already frustrated feelings of how that night was going with him.

So we finally get to show time, and we have a pretty small crowd on hand of maybe 50 people, but they were very vocal and lively for a smallish sized crowd. All the matches went pretty well that night, with the exception of me breaking my right finger in my match with Steve's *Mr. X* character. It hurt like a son of a gun, but there is not much they can do for a broken finger other than put it in a splint. Afterwards, Larry complimented me on my match and the new ring attire that I had worn, but he never bothered apologizing to me for the disrespect he showed me earlier that day. But I guess Larry's compliment was as close to an apology as I was going to get from him, as he was just that kind of guy. It was at this event that I noticed the change that was taking place in Steve Engstrom. Steve had been with us since March of 1985, and he was always one of my best right-hand guys. In the past, I could always rely on him for anything it seemed. And I always felt we were good friends. But now he had started to hang around with Larry and his older buddies all of the time. And it seemed as if the rest of us were just second rate to him now. And it started to bother me, *a lot*.

We were now in the middle of winter, and we had no place to tape new shows from, which we needed to do to fill our weekly timeslots. So knowing I was getting desperate, Larry and Steve decided to approach me with a proposition. Larry said he knew of a large pole barn that we could use to keep our ring set up in. We could use the place to do our weekly shows from and practice as well. I figured great, let's do it. Only Steve and Larry had one little hitch. For them letting me use this location, they wanted to make some changes in how we were operating. For starters, Steve and Larry wanted to break away from the NWF and form their own league called the NCWA. This league would be comprised of all their older counterparts and would be a lot more similar to what Eddie Sharkey was doing with the PWA. They still wanted to work with me as far as doing live public cards and whatnot, but we would each be in charge of our own leagues respectively. This way, Larry could run his NCWA league himself instead of having to answer to me. Secondly, they wanted me to drop the entire lightweight division of the NWF and only use the bigger kids.

This whole thing was beginning to stink, and I did not like any of it. I was feeling very betrayed by Steve as he was siding with Larry on this whole situation. The term *loyalty* did not mean a thing to Steve Engstrom. But we were in a tough spot, and I had always been a realist. In order to get the location and keep doing the shows, we had to comply with what they wanted. So even though I strongly objected to it, I agreed to release the NWF's lightweight division. This meant that wrestlers such as *The Super Ds* (Todd and Troy Dusosky), *Rough Ryan* (Ryan Kelsey), *The Blade Runners* (Todd and Troy Sufka), Terry Kosnapal, and others were released from the league. These guys were the heart and soul of our league, and it just killed me to have to do this. Getting rid of them was something I would regret for many years to come.

As we started off the year doing our TV tapings from the new pole barn location, which was located in Dayton, MN, we had a few new faces join the league. David Dixon brought in Jamie McParland, who at first was calling himself *The Irish Terror*. Jamie had actually attended our Brooklyn Park armory event back in December, and as you watched that tape, you would see this kid running around ringside getting very vocal with all the action. In fact, at one point he actually jumped into the ring at the end of one of the matches. That was Jamie. But one thing about Jamie was that he was a natural when it came to doing professional wrestling. He was able to take the bumps as if he had been doing it for years, and this was not a common thing with most newcomers. Other newcomers included the trio of *The Destructors*, consisting of John Hoffman, Gary Parr, and Leslie Johnson, who was also referred to as *The Mystery Man*. These guys were like a Road Warriors-type of team. In addition to them, a few new guys that Larry brought in were Ken Boyer and Bobby Pfeifer. Ken served as a match commentator and announcer. Bobby was Larry's on-screen manager, where he went by the name *Beautiful Bobby Ferrari*.

Invader I suplexes The Irish Terror from a TV Taping in 1987.

PRO WRESTLING KIDS' STYLE

As far as the NCWA went, they had Steve and Larry and an initial cast that consisted of Ernie Ellis (*Dirty Ernie*), Jeff Dinsmore (*Dr. Dread*), and a few others that went by the stage names of *Grizzly Stevens, The Hornet, Captain Caveman,* and perhaps a few more that I cannot remember. Also, Ken Boyer and Bobby Pfeifer formed a tag team called *The Unknown Studs.* But Larry did not want them in his league as a tag team, so I had them compete in the NWF instead. Also, since the fall of 1986, we had been doing a special 30-minute talk show on Saturdays, which we called *The NWF's Saturday Afternoon Special.* On this show, I was the host, and we would have several guest wrestlers from the wrestling show come on each week. And around the first of the year, I asked Bobby to become my co-host with me, which he did. Bobby was a nice guy behind the scenes, and I always got along with him. And together, we made a great team hosting that Saturday show.

Mike Bauer and Chris Barger approached me at the first of the year and said they no longer wanted to be a part of the NWF *producers council.* They did not like the direction we were going and the relationship we had with Steve and Larry's NCWA. They did want to continue on as wrestlers on the show, though, which I was cool with. And both Mike and Chris both warned me about Steve and Larry and suggested I be very careful in dealing with them. I knew where they were coming from, but at the time, I felt I could handle the whole situation.

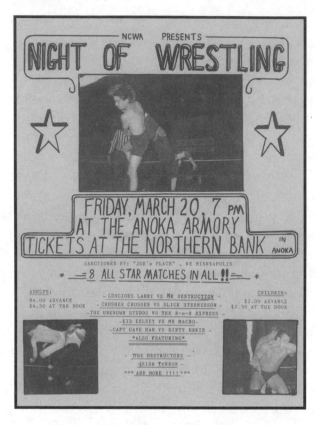

Actual flyer for the NWF/NCWA Anoka Armory
card in March of 1987.

Also around this time, we booked the Anoka Armory for what would be our second dual promotional card with both the NWF and the NCWA. I used our money we had in the NWF to pay for the armory, buy all the advertising, print up tickets and so forth. Larry and Steve contributed nothing for the event, other than about four or five matches to be held on the card from their league. The first card would be held just prior to this event at a place called The Dri Dock, which was a nonalcoholic nightclub. Jeff Dinsmore set it up, as he was a good friend with the owner of the place. I started to promote both of these events on our weekly shows as well.

So as we start off in 1987, I was really torn at all that was going on with our league. On the one hand, I was glad to have a good location to tape from and do our weekly shows, but having to work side by side with Steve and Larry and their NCWA league was not the most comfortable thing. I was beginning to wonder if Steve and Larry were not just using me to get exposure on our weekly cable show? As much as I didn't like the relationship, I felt it was the only choice we had to keep our league alive. As we approached the March armory event, advance ticket sales were decent, and it looked as though we were going to have a good-sized crowd on hand. We also had some exciting matches lined up as well. But little did we know then just how exciting that night would turn out to be, as we were in for a real surprise.

Chapter 17
A Low Blow

So on the arrival of March 20th, 1987, we made our return to the Anoka Armory in an event featuring matches from the NWF and the NCWA billed as *Night Of Wrestling*. And as the doors opened for the event, we had a good-sized line forming outside. We ended up having about 375 people in attendance that night—not quite a sellout, but pretty darn close.

As for the NWF, we had some really good matches on this card. Our newest and hottest team of *The Destructors* went up against *Invade I* and *Invader III* (*Invader III* was now Jamie McParland's new wrestling name). This was an awesome match with all four doing great moves to decent fan reaction. We had *The Unknown Studs* (Boyer and Pfeifer) taking on *The Rack-n-Roll Express* (Barger and Bauer) for the NWF World Tag Team Titles, and this was another great match with lots of highflying action. Then we had *Kid "USA" Kelsey* up against *Mr. Macho* in one of their countless battles from their ongoing feud. And then there was myself, *Crusher Crossen*, defending my NWF World Title against *Slick Steenerson* in a special match where in order for me to win, I had to body slam Steenerson. We called it a "no slam, no belt" match.

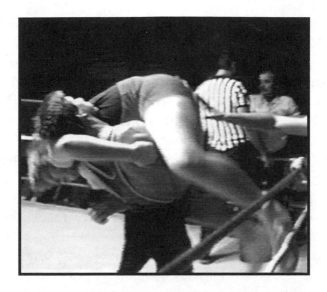

Crossen slams Steenerson from the Anoka Armory in March of 1987.

What was interesting about this match with Steenerson was that Troy actually weighed 250 pounds, for *real*. And at that time, I was only 145 pounds myself. Now I was supposed to win this match by body slamming Troy, but when we practiced it a week or so prior, Troy was too heavy for me to be able to do it. As much as we rehearsed it, I just could not get him over convincingly. So we worked out this little routine where I would get close to the ropes, and as I went to do the body slam on Troy, his partner *Mr. Macho* (who would be at ringside) would jump up on the apron and pretend to attempt to hold Troy from getting slammed, but in reality he would actually be pushing Troy over so I could get him slammed. It was the only way we could pull it off. So towards the end of the actual match, Troy and I got close to the ropes, and I went to do the slam. *Mr. Macho* jumped up on the apron to do his part, only Troy and I were too far away from the ropes, but we didn't know it. What happened next was I actually body slammed Troy all on my own. How I managed to do that I would never know, but somehow I did it and only after watching the tapes afterwards did we see that *Mr. Macho* was of no help at all.

As for the NCWA, I cannot even remember what matches they had that night other than *Luscious Larry* taking on *Derek Dukes* for the main event. But to be honest, I thought that our NWF matches were a heck of a lot more entertaining than theirs. And then again, that is just my opinion, I guess. The card was OK in general, but I really missed not having our lightweight kids like *Rough Ryan* and *The Super Ds* on hand, as they were big-time crowd favorites at our armory events in the past, and not having them there was like not having a missing piece to a puzzle it seemed.

At the end of the night, I was feeling pretty good. And as I was in the locker room picking up a few things, Matt Kelsey rushed in and said that Larry and Steve had just taken off with the cash box from the gate sales as well as the wrestling ring itself, which they had previously loaded up. I remember I yelled out, "They did *what?*" And as I quickly walked out of the dressing room into the now-empty armory, all I saw was the empty floor with debris left from that night's card and a few folding chairs, and that was it. And just like Matt said, Steve and Larry and the rest of the NCWA guys had split taking all the proceeds from that night's card with them and leaving us with absolutely nothing. Out of all the things I had ever gotten angry about regarding this wrestling business, I was never madder than at that exact moment. *How could they just double-cross us like that?* I thought. And Steve, how could he turn on us and just backstab us like this? At the time, I was absolutely furious, and the more I thought about it, the madder I got. The only thing we were left with was all the video footage from the event itself. I remember that as the rest of us left the armory that night, I was with Mike Whaley (*Mr. Macho*), Matt Kelsey (*Kid Kelsey*), and Troy Steenerson (*Slick Steenerson*). And we all kept talking about how bad Steve and Larry double-crossed us on this whole thing. Here we had put up all the money for the event and did all the advertising work, and in the end Steve and Larry just walked off with all the proceeds from the event that night. But what *really* had me angry was the fact that they took our wrestling ring. And whether they liked it or not, that ring belonged to the NWF.

The next day I called up Steve and asked him what the hell happened the night before, and I remember him acting dumb as if he didn't have anything to do with it. I then went on to tell him that the wrestling ring needs to be returned to us as soon as possible. I gave him a 24-hour deadline. After 24 hours passed and still no ring in sight, I decided to call the police. You see, back when we purchased the wrestling ring, I had every piece of it serialized with the Anoka Police Department. Steve never knew I did that, and I did it just in case the ring would ever get stolen. Well, in this case, Steve and Larry *stole* our wrestling ring. So once the police were involved, then Steve and Larry wanted to talk.

I remember we set up a meeting at my house, where I was with my mom and Troy Steenerson. And Steve showed up with Larry's father (because Larry was working second shift, I guess). Larry's dad did all the talking for him and Steve. They tried to argue that Steve actually had part of the ownership of the ring since he contributed money to help pay for it originally. But I quickly pointed out that Steve did that voluntarily while he was a part of the NWF, and that our NWF organization was the only rightful owner of that ring. Once they realized they were not going to win that argument, they offered to buy me out so they could keep the ring. Larry's dad wanted to write me a check right then and there. And I refused any amount they offered. I told them that I want that ring returned within two days or else I would be pressing charges. For me, it was now just a matter of principle, and I did not want them to get off easy by simply flashing some cash. So not having anything else they could say, they agreed to return the wrestling ring to us that following day. And as for the money they walked off with the night of the event, they claimed that after paying the Armory costs and other talent used that night, that there was nothing left to spare. I knew that was a bunch of bull. But because I could not prove how much money was in the cash box that night, there was nothing I could do about the lost proceeds. As they left, they were not the happiest campers, but I could have cared less how they felt. My mom had started laying into Steve as well by telling him what a traitor he was for turning his back on me like he did, and Steve just sat there with his head down like some guilty two-year old does when he knows he has done wrong. The next day, they returned the ring to my garage just like they said they would.

So we got the ring back, but we were completely broke and had nowhere to set the ring up at in order to use it for our weekly shows. I could not even sneak it in my backyard anymore, because the following week we were moving into a new townhouse across town. Besides all of that, the last few months of dealing with the whole Steve and Larry thing had really drained me. And I personally needed a break from it all. So for the first time in nearly four years, I stopped producing the NWF weekly wrestling show, both locally and nationally. And for the time being, the NWF Kids Pro Wrestling Show was temporarily at a standstill. It was April of 1987.

During that summer, I had become pretty good friends with Jamie McParland, and Jamie kept bugging me to start the NWF back up again. But at the time, I just did not have the ambition to do it, or the location for that matter. But I did convince Jamie to start his own league, which he called the CWF. I even told him that I would defend my NWF World Title on his show once he got it up and running. He ended up getting a lot of the old kids that we used to have on our show, such as Terry Kosnapal, Chris Downs (*The Ice Dragon*), Chris Hanson (*Sgt. Smash*), and others. So as he was starting that up, I would help him out with advice and such, but I did not want to actually go there and do any of the work for him. This was his show, and I wanted him to be able to accomplish all of it on his own, that way it would mean more to him in the end.

Jamie McParland during an NWF interview from early 1987.

So as Jamie was getting his league off the ground, I got a call from Greg Buschman and Scott Dotzler. These were the two guys that I used as my production crew to handle the remote cameras at ringside during our armory events. As it turned out, they were now certified to check out the mobile van unit. This was basically like a production studio on wheels, as it was equipped with three cameras. They wanted to know if I would be interested in doing another NWF armory card again, so they could use the mobile van to produce the entire event for us. Now this was very tempting. I started to think about how awesome the final product would look coming from the mobile van production truck. This was just the kind of motivation I was looking for. And so as I thought about it, I told them I would get back to them. I then called Matt, Jason, Mike, Troy, and Jamie to see what they all thought about doing another armory event. Needless to say, they were all for it, big-time. So after talking to them and further convincing myself, I called back Scott and Greg and told them that the Anoka Armory was a go, and I would get them a date in a few days. As hard as it was to believe, the NWF was actually going to promote a live show at the Anoka Armory, once again.

—

Chapter 18
Superstars Spectacular '87

After having those few months off, I felt totally revitalized. It gave me just the break I needed, and now I felt I had the energy to once again get things back on track again with our league. It was in the middle of June, so I set the date for the armory card for August 23rd, 1987. This way we would have a good two months to actually promote it. The second thing I did was I got our weekly show back on the air, since we had been off the air for about two months now. What we used for wrestling footage was rehashed matches from 1986 and early 1987 with updated interview segments to start promoting our upcoming armory event. We were calling it *Superstars Spectacular '87*, making it a sequel to our very first armory event, for which I had always wanted that venue to be an annual event anyway. So the title was perfect.

Actual flyer for the Anoka Armory card in August of 1987.

Then we got posters and tickets printed up, and we went to work on getting the posters up as much as we could around town. But because we had been off the air for so long, I still felt we needed to do more. So I looked into running some cable TV ads for our area, which covered the north side of the Twin Cities suburbs. Back then in those pre-satellite years, cable TV had a commanding market share. And what was nice was that the cable ads could be placed on specific stations such as MTV, USA, ESPN, etc. But even more importantly, they could be placed during specific programs. So I got to thinking, why not have the ads run during *AWA Championship Wrestling* on ESPN, *World Championship Wrestling* on TBS, and *WWF Prime Time Wrestling* on the USA network. So we purchased a $500 block of advertising through Group W Cable for a territory that covered nearly half of the Twin Cities in a geographical coverage area. And I made sure our ad would fall during those specific wrestling programs that were airing on those specific networks. Out of all my ideas, I always thought that this one was one of the best I ever thought of. It takes the term *direct marketing* to a whole new level.

But getting the $500 to pay for it was another story. We barely had enough money to cover the armory down payment and initial advertising costs. So knowing that both Greg Buschman and Scott Dotzler had money available, I convinced them both to invest in the event by fronting the money for the advertising. And if we would have a profitable event, then I would give them a 200 percent return. Meaning they could double their money. It was a great deal for them. But I told them that there is always the risk that we would not bring in enough money on the day of the event, if ticket sales were bad. But I then reminded them that our cable ads would be inserted during the regular wrestling programs on primetime TV, so how could we go wrong with that? They agreed to do it, and so we started running these ads about 10 days prior to the event.

As far as getting kids back on the show, I had Jamie McParland and few of his CWF guys such as Terry Kosnapal and Chris Downs (*The Ice Dragon*). We also brought back Troy Otto (*Bull Dog Batcher*), Chad Rancour (*Dr. Destruction*), all three of *The Destructors* including *The Mystery Man*, Mike Bauer, and Chris Barger (*Rack-n-Roll Express*), along with other past wrestlers like Ken Boyer and Bob Pfeifer (*The Unknown Studs*), Tim Holland and Jerry Wellman (*The Barbarians*), Mike Whaley (*Mr. Macho*), Troy Steenerson (*Slick Steenerson*), Matt Kelsey (*Kid Kelsey*), and myself, *Crusher Crossen*. We had a few debuts, including John Hoffman's younger brother Joe Hoffman who went by the name *The Disco Kid,* and Tommy Katnis, who called himself *Tommy Tornado Katnis.* All in all, we had a pretty decent bunch of guys to work with, and it looked as though the event would be a promising one.

The original "Destructors" from early 1987.

With a few days to go before the event, I noticed that our advance ticket sales were not doing so great. What I was not aware of was that the NWA was also holding a major card on the same day over at *The Met Center* in Bloomington, MN. And not that it mattered, but Larry's NCWA league was also having a card the same day as us too. But I did not let it worry me. Either way, we were going to do this armory card.

On the day of the event, Mike Whaley went out of his way to rent a limo—using his own money. He then invited Matt Kelsey, Jerry Wellman, Troy Steenerson, Jason Clauson, and myself out to eat. So before the event, we all had a steak dinner and then made our return back to the armory in the limo. But because we were enemies in the ring, some of us had to get dropped off separately. The entire limo exposure outside the armory made for great PR that night just before the event started. But I would later learn that Tim Holland was a little upset that he was not invited in the limo while his cousin Jerry was.

So as we start the event, we only had about 70 people in attendance, and this was mainly due to the NWA event that was taking place across town. But the fans that were there were ready for action. We opened it up with Terry Kosnapal against *The Disco Kid*. This match was an excellent one, as Terry was a great up-and-comer for our league. Then we had *The Destructors* against *Bull Dog Butcher* and Tommy Katnis. We had been trying to get Tommy to join the league from the very beginning back in 1984, so it's funny that now nearly four years later, he finally made his debut. The match was good and had a lot of action in it. Next we had *The Ice Dragon* and *The Mystery Man* up against *Invader III* (McParland) and *The White Ninja* (Mike Whaley in a mask). Chad Rancour was supposed to be Chris Downs' partner, but he was late in arriving so we had to have Leslie (*The Mystery Man*) fill in for him. Chris Downs (*Ice Dragon*) had actually broken his wrist about three weeks earlier, so we had him use his cast as a foreign object during the match to get the win.

For the next match, it was supposed to be *The Rack-n-Roll Express* against *The Unknown Studs*. But about 15 minutes prior to their match, I found out that Steve Engstrom had shown up to take Bob Pfeifer's place as one of the *Studs*. I was not happy with this at all, as I was still very bitter towards Steve for what he had done with the whole NCWA deal a few months back. But I was not about to get into it with him on such short notice before their match. But just seeing him there again made me want to puke. Then I had my title match against Kelsey. This match was the event's big one since we had been partners for the last two years, and in the past month, I had Kelsey turn on me to build up a feud between us. The match went well with just one small problem. With Kelsey, whenever I would attempt my flying drop kick on him, he used to always back away too early, and it always looked like I had missed him by a mile. So during that match when I went to do my flying drop kick on him, I made sure I got a little bit closer than usual, and this time Matt decided not to back away either. The end result was a perfect flying drop kick right to his face. But the bad thing was it wound up dislocating his jaw. I must say as I watched it afterwards, it looked great on tape. Then we had *Slick Steenerson* and *Mr. Macho* take on *The Barbarians* for the Tag Team titles. The match was decent and full of high power moves.

Crossen dropkicks Kelsey from the Anoka Armory in 1987.

The final match for the night was a battle royal, and that was where everything went haywire. I was supposed to win that match, but because Tim Holland was still bitter about not being invited out to dinner with us, he decided to take it out on me. As we got to the end of the battle royal, I was left in the ring with Tim, and his two cousins Jerry and Chad. I soon came to realize that the three of them were not going to allow me to win the battle royal, as they started ganging up on me for real. Their game plan was simple— just keep me from winning the match. What could I have done? It was a three-on-one situation, and so I held out for as long as I could. But, after a while, I knew it was going nowhere, so I had no choice but to let them just throw me out. It was a pretty lame and selfish thing to do on their part, and I was pretty upset about it afterwards.

Once I got into the back dressing room, all the guys started asking me what just happened as they had been watching it from the monitor, and so I told them what they basically already knew. Once Tim, Jerry, and company got into the dressing room, they had the rest of the guys so ticked off for pulling that stunt that we nearly had a fight break out in the locker room. The *entire* league was on their case in my defense, telling the three of them how disrespectful they were to do what they just did. This only added to Tim's childish and feverish temper, and so we more or less told him to get his stuff and get out. I told him he was finished, and that this was the *last* time he would ever work another NWF card again. Later I remember John Hoffman telling me that they knew what was happening in the dressing room during the match, and that they were considering about having all the guys in the locker room come out and rush the ring and throw the three of them out of the battle royal. I told him that I wished they would have done that.

But other than that incident, the event went very well. We could have used a few more people there that night, but with the NWA in town, what could you say? Steve did tell me that Larry's NCWA card earlier that day had even fewer people than we did, so that made me feel like we had succeeded. I never did get Greg or Scott's money back for them on their advertising investment they made. They were pretty disappointed about it, but they also were aware of the risks involved all along. So, in the end, they had no gripes about it. On the brighter side, this was our first mobile van production, and the quality of the finished production was better than I could have ever imagined. And with the use of the van, Scott and Greg did a great job in handling the technical production of the event. But most of all, it felt good to be back in the ring again. And the rest of the guys all agreed on that. But the following month I would be presented with an opportunity from a blast from the past that would once again, change everything.

Chapter 19
The Final Bell

After the August armory card, as much as I enjoyed getting back in the ring again like the rest of the guys, I still was not prepared to run the show full steam ahead like before. There were a lot of reasons for that, mainly due to the fact that we were now living in a townhouse in Columbia Heights, and I just did not have any location where I could set up the ring at. And it was shortly after this time that I received a call from Ernie Ellis, one of the guys from the NCWA league. Back in the days when we were all working together, I got to know all the guys fairly well from the NCWA. And as it turned out, most of them had a falling out with Larry over the past month or two, and so Ernie wanted to meet with me to discuss a proposition.

So we met at The Dri Dock, the same place we held our first-ever NWF/NCWA dual card at back in March of 1987. When I showed up, Ernie was there with Jeff Dinsmore, another former NCWA guy. They both went on to tell me how Larry had started working with Jim Mitchell and that the two of them had basically shafted most all of the original NCWA guys out of the league. Then Ernie told me that he had heard that I was not that much interested in continuing on with the NWF, and so he wanted to know if I would be interested in selling the league to him. Jeff Dinsmore then said that they would be able to hold monthly events there at The Dri Dock where we would be able to maintain a weekly show with for cable TV. They then went on to say that they wanted me to be in charge of the entire television

128

production, as far as producing the cable TV program. But my main concern was what would happen to all of the kids in our current NWF league? And Ernie and Jeff both assured me that they would keep them all on, and that they would have a mix of adults and kids, just as before when we did those dual cards in the past.

But the real question here was *trust*. Could I *trust* these guys? Although I had always gotten along with them in the past, meeting them both and discussing a possible buyout was a lot like making a deal with the devil. It was a situation that could go either way. If they were honest and true to their word, it would be great for our league. But on the other hand if they were to go back on their promises, then it would be disastrous for our league. So I gave it some serious thought. The rest of the kids such as Jamie, Matt, Jason, and Troy all wanted me to just keep the league in my control, as they did not trust Ernie or Jeff. But I wanted to get on with my life and be less dependent on everyone else in running the league. I was nearly 18 years old now, and I really needed to start thinking about my future.

So after giving it a lot of thought, I agreed to sell the league to Ernie and work with him in both maintaining the weekly cable show and serving as a wrestler on the show as well. In the buyout for $500, which covered the value of the ring, they agreed to keep the name the same, so it was still going to be called NWF Wrestling. Right away, we went to work on setting up our first big card at The Dri Dock, which we were dubbing as *Wrestle-Vision*. The date for that event was set for October 27th, 1987. We did several interview segments to promote it, and we had a great bunch of guys from both the NWF and NCWA set to appear.

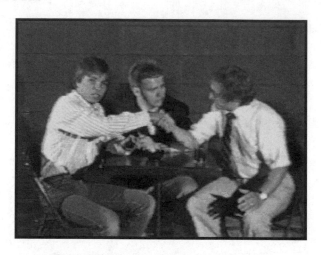

*Shawn "Crusher" Crossen, Jason Clauson,
and Jeff Dinmore from the fall of 1987.*

For the NWF, we had a rematch signed for the NWF World Title between *Kid Kelsey* and myself. We also had *Mr. Macho* and *Slick Steenerson* defending their NWF tag team title belts. We had *The Destructors*, Jamie McParland, who was now going by his new wrestling name of *Ricky Vaun*, and *The Ice Dragon*. For the old NCWA guys, we had *Dirty Ernie, Dr. Dread*, and *Grizzly Stevens*. Another guy that was coming in from the old NCWA was Steve Engstrom. I wasn't too thrilled about his return as we both had never been the same with each other since the fallout we had back in March, but I felt I could tolerate him. The thing with Steve was he was always so full of hot air all the time that you never knew what to believe from him. I remember him trying to tell all of us that he had been working for several independent promotions during the past six months all over the country and up in Canada. Yeah sure, *right* Steve. You just had to let it go in one ear and out the other with this guy.

Since I was in charged of overseeing the cable TV production, I had Greg Buschman and Scott Dotzler set to direct the technical production that night by using the mobile van unit to tape the entire event. As we approached show time, the place was packed. We had to have nearly 200 people in there, and The Dri Dock is not the biggest place around, so it was very tight seating. And for this being the first card with the new NWF, everything seemed to go pretty smoothly. That first event was a lot of fun because we were using a true mix of the old NWF and the old NCWA, and we all worked together in perfect harmony that night. All the matches were solid, and the fan reaction could not have been any better, the entire event went over perfectly. If only the rest of the cards at The Dri Dock that followed this first one would have gone just as smoothly, but that wish would soon prove to be false.

In the months that followed that first event, Ernie and company slowly filtered and phased out all of the mainstay kids from the NWF until there was just Jamie and myself left from the original NWF.. And so after going through all of that and seeing what the league had become, there was one missing ingredient from the whole thing, and that was "fun." It just wasn't *fun* anymore. Back when we were doing the kids pro wrestling show, we were having so much fun with it. But now, all of us kids were nearly adults, and we lost the entire concept that made us so unique in the first place. So with the fun of it now gone, on May 15th, 1988, I decided to retire from the NWF. This, however, would not be my last appearance in the wrestling ring.

For the remainder on 1988, I remained close friends with Troy Steenerson. By 1989, we were talking about how much we missed the actual wrestling show. Also, we heard that Ernie was no longer running the NWF anymore, and so we asked him if he would be interested in selling back the wrestling ring. He agreed to sell it back (for $500,) and we bought it. We were not sure what exactly we were going to do with it, but Troy had a large pole barn out at his house, so we set the ring up there and did a few pilot shows with a few of the old guys from the NWF. Then, the next thing that happened is something we never expected.

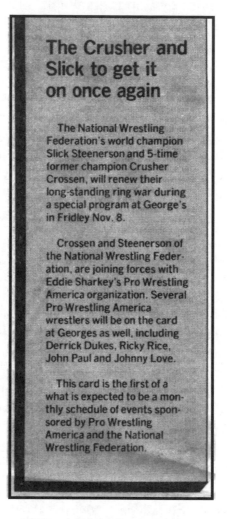

The Crusher and Slick to get it on once again

The National Wrestling Federation's world champion Slick Steenerson and 5-time former champion Crusher Crossen, will renew their long-standing ring war during a special program at George's in Fridley Nov. 8.

Crossen and Steenerson of the National Wrestling Federation, are joining forces with Eddie Sharkey's Pro Wrestling America organization. Several Pro Wrestling America wrestlers will be on the card at Georges as well, including Derrick Dukes, Ricky Rice, John Paul and Johnny Love.

This card is the first of a what is expected to be a monthly schedule of events sponsored by Pro Wrestling America and the National Wrestling Federation.

Write-up in ABC newspapers
regarding Crossen & Steenerson and the PWA.

I got a call from Eddie Sharkey, and he wanted to know if Troy and myself would be interested in working some dates with him on his PWA promotion. I had remained good friends with Eddie over the years, and so I asked Troy what he thought about it. We agreed that it would be a smart decision, so over the course of a few months, we worked about three or four dates with Eddie at George's Nightclub in Fridley, MN. Both Troy and I went over well in the PWA, getting decent fan reaction. And in time, we would both capture the PWA Middleweight title. I remember there was this new kid in town that started to work in the PWA shortly after Troy and I joined. His wrestling name was *The Lightning Kid,* while his real name was Sean Waltman. In January of 1990, I moved 200 miles away into Wisconsin, so I was unable to make every date at George's from that point on. And it seemed that on the dates when I would be signed to wrestle, Waltman would not be, and vice-versa, so I never met him myself. But I do remember Troy telling me about this new kid that was in town—how he looked just like me, that he had a similar ring style, and he even had the same name as I did. Because we were so similar, Troy said that all the guys in the locker room were getting him confused for me. Ray Webbie, one of the PWA promoters at the time, was planning on setting up a match between Waltman and myself. The match was going to be setup for an annual fund raiser they did every year called *Wrestle For Shelter.* Ray approached me and asked if I would be interested in working a match with Sean for that event? Of course, I had no objections to it and I looked forward to working with him in the ring. Steve Engstrom was also making his presence known in the PWA, only now he was acting as Troy's ringside manager. Even though I didn't care for Steve anymore, Troy had always remained friends with him.

*Slick Steenerson and Crusher Crossen
in a PWA promo shot from 1989.*

Sometime in the spring of 1990, I began to hear some disturbing rumors that were floating around. According to Troy, Eddie was unhappy with me since I could no longer make every match while living in Wisconsin. So I decided to give Eddie a call to discuss my situation, and I figured he would understand it if I could just explain it to him over the phone. So I got a hold of Eddie and started to talk to him, but I noticed him being very short with me during the conversation. This was not like the Eddie that I knew, so I figured something was up. And as we continued our conversation, he started to get angry with me. Eventually, he told me that I was finished in the PWA, and he hung up the phone on me. At first I could not believe what I was hearing. I was in a state of disbelief. I had been nothing but a true and loyal friend to Eddie Sharkey for the past four years. Why was he all of a sudden treating me like this now? I could never understand why Eddie so abruptly changed his feelings towards me. I mean, one day we were good friends and the next thing I know, he wanted me gone for good. I always wondered if Steve didn't have something to do with that, by talking to Eddie about me behind my back. Steve was good for that kind of stuff, and I could see him doing that with Eddie. To this day it remains a mystery. But whatever the reason was with Eddie, there was no changing his mind about it. So with that, the upcoming scheduled match between *Crusher Crossen* and *The Lightning Kid* was canceled. And April 16th, 1990, would mark my final match in professional wrestling. I was the current PWA Middleweight Champion at the time, and to this day I still have that belt.

Chapter 20
An Everlasting Experience

So now you're probably thinking that this whole story ends on a real sour note with what happened to me in the PWA, right? Wrong. It really doesn't. You see my experience with the PWA is similar to what happens in the *real* world of professional wrestling on a regular basis. What Eddie Sharkey did to me was nothing new in the wrestling game, as several others before me have been dealt the same hand. I certainly was not the first, nor will I ever be the last, that has had to deal with anything like that. In the wrestling business, that is unfortunately a common experience.

But let's talk about what was *not* a common experience. In 1984, it was not common for a bunch of kids to get together and start their own pro wrestling show. It certainly was not common for any kid to have the drive to keep doing it for several years steady in producing cable TV shows each and every week. It was not common for a kid to be able to overcome adversities of all different magnitudes over that time. It was definitely not common for a kid to promote live public wrestling events at school gymnasiums and National Guard armories, where hundreds would pay admission to see their shows. And it was not common for kids of this venue to get on the local news stations and in local newspapers all with positive community support.

So my memories don't focus on my common experience with the PWA in 1990, but more so on the uncommon experiences I had from 1984 through 1988 with the NWF. Those were some incredible years for me. As you look back at the true history of professional wrestling, how many situations can you find in the early 1980s that even remotely resembled what we did with NWF Kids Pro Wrestling? The answer is pretty simple—there were none. We were the only ones. We were the true pioneers of do-it-yourself professional wrestling. And most rewarding of all, we did it all on our own, where our only help came from each other.

Back at the height of our success, I always wondered why the media thought we were so interesting to do stories about. *Why us?* I thought. What makes us so special? We were just a bunch of kids having fun with our wrestling show, or so I thought. So at the time, while I appreciated the extra publicity, I could never really understand why the media was so interested with us in the first place. And only now that I have gotten a lot older can I see just what the media had seen in us back then. And that was the fact that you just don't have many kids that have the drive or ambition that it takes to run a league like I was doing. That was in itself, something special and unique, and the media could see that. Over time, most kids would have lost interest in an endeavor such as this, yet I stayed focused on running it for nearly five years, and that was why the media found us so unique.

The main thing to remember about our wrestling show was that, at the time, nobody else was doing anything like it. Nowadays, you have kids doing what they call *backyard wrestling* all the time. Leagues like that are basically a dime a dozen. And the sad thing about them is that most of them are extremely unorganized and somewhat dangerous. And in most cases, they usually get negative press coverage as well. But as common as *backyard wrestling* has become today, back in the mid-80s, I can assure you that we were the only ones out there. In fact, the term *backyard wrestling* did not even exist in those days, and we never considered ourselves as such.

In those four to five years in the mid-80s while running my wrestling show as a kid, I learned more about fundamental life experiences than I had ever thought possible. I learned how to solve problems, no matter how big the adversities were. I learned how to promote and advertise an event, and what makes them succeed and what makes them fail. I learned how to lead and organize a group of kids from the ground up becoming more successful than any of us could have ever imagined. I learned how to successfully run a business, and how to deal with other people in making that business work. There is not a college on the face of this earth that could have ever prepared me any better for life than the NWF Kids Pro Wrestling Show, and *that* is a fact.

People have often asked me if I regret what happened between myself and Eddie and the PWA, in that perhaps I missed out on a possible gateway opportunity into the real world of professional wrestling. And the answer to that is quite simply, NO. Because if that is the way the real world of professional wrestling operates, then I don't want any part of it. I enjoyed the years doing our NWF Kids Pro Wrestling Show because it was fun, and we learned from it, and we grew from it. But with the PWA, the only thing that I learned was how to betray your friends and colleagues in a world of egos and unfounded politics. So if I had to choose between having my kids pro wrestling show or landing some contract in the world of professional wrestling? I would take doing my kids pro wrestling show a hundred times over. But hey, that's just me.

And if I have a message that I want some 14-year-old kid to understand, it is this … No matter what the situation is that you want to do. No matter how high the odds are stacked up against you. No matter how little you have in order to accomplish it. Always remember this, there is nothing … and I mean *nothing* … that you cannot accomplish if you put your mind to it. And if you should ever doubt that statement, just read this book again and let my experience become your inspiration. That is something that all of us should never forget, that if you put your mind to it, you really can make your dreams come true. I am living proof of that.

Chapter 21
Where Are They Now?

It has been nearly 20 years since we did the wrestling show, and perhaps the biggest question I get from everyone that learns our story is … What ever happened to everyone? And that can be a very tough question. To be perfectly honest, I just never stayed in touch with everyone that was in the show over all these years. You have to understand that when I had my bad dealings with Eddie Sharkey back in 1990 when he told me to pack my bags, I was so fed up with the wrestling business at that time that I wanted nothing to do with it. So for years I would just avoid the entire wrestling picture and that meant distancing myself from most all of the guys from our show as it only reminded me of what I was trying to forget.

Of course today I really regret doing that because now I miss those days of our original NWF and I certainly miss the camaraderie I had with all the guys. But in 1990, I felt that I needed to forget the past and just move on. Needless to say, I did not shut out everyone. I remained close friends with a few of the guys and just recently I have came into contact with several of the others. And after all these years, it's amazing to find out that all the guys still remember the NWF and all the fun we had.

The last time I actually saw Mike Ackerrmann (Merciless Mike) was when he showed up at the Anoka Armory back in 1986, but I understand he is happily married and living in Eastern

Wisconsin. Today, Mike makes his living as an optometrist where he does LASIK eye surgeries. I last spoke with Mike on the phone back in 1998, and we shared a few old memories from the show. It was great to speak with him and I made sure to tell him how much I appreciated everything he did for our show back in the 1980s. And talking with him was just like old times.

Mike Ackermann.

Rob Jacob (Jackknife Jacob) now lives out on the east coast. I am not completely sure what he does but someone told me they thought he works with the stock market. If it's true, it does not surprise me. Rob always had a good head on his shoulders and working with the stock market would be a perfect job for him to be able to handle. I have tried to track Rob down again after all these years but because of his common name, it has been next to impossible.

Chris Daniels (Tuffer Daniels) still lives in the Twin Cities area of Minnesota and is a sporting goods representative. He is married and spends a lot of time traveling with his job. I recently contacted him through the email to find that he still goes by his nickname of "Tuffer".

Matt Kelsey (Kid USA Kelsey) currently lives in Woodbury, MN. He lives with his fiancé and will be getting married in early 2005. Matt went to school for business accounting and that is what he does at present. The last time I actually saw Matt was back in 1989, but we have stayed in touch over the phone through out the years. Every time we talk to each other, we always reminisce over that famous dropkick from the last match we had with each other at the Anoka Armory.

Matt Kelsey.

Ever since the falling out I had with Steve Engstrom (Mr. X and Pretty Boy Taylor), we have never been the same with each other. Besides having to deal with him during my PWA years in 1989 and 1990, I had seen him one other time around 1992 at a house party in Anoka. Steve tried to patch things up with me somewhat that night, but I will never forget what he done to our league back in 1987, the way he just turned his back on us. A few years later, I heard that Steve was spending time in the county correctional facilities and it did not surprise me.

As for his sidekick Larry Rhode (Luscious Larry), I have no idea what ever happened to him, nor do I really care to find out.

Jason Clauson (Corporal Clauson) still lives in the Twin Cities. He is running a couple very successful businesses up in Anoka. He handles his fathers business of garage doors as well as a new landscaping supply company, and he is doing well. I saw Jason for the first time in 15 years in 2004 where we met and had a drink up in Coon Rapids, MN. It was great to see Jason again, and share a few old memories.

Jason Clauson.

Chris and Jay Downs (The Ice Dragon and The Fly) still live in the Twin Cities as well, and I have been in touch with both by way of email. I have also talked with Chris over the phone recently, and they both are doing well. Jay had gone into the navy after high school, but is no longer active. Chris spends most of his free time with his daughter who I believe is around nine years old. Chris and I both joke around with each other about setting up a rematch with each other, and this time have it in a steel cage! That's just what the wrestling world needs to see, Crusher Crossen against The Ice Dragon, one more time.

Chris Hanson (Sgt. Smash) now is happily married living in Ramsey, MN and has his hands full with his young daughter. Chris is the one I speak with the most as of late, and he surely misses the old days just like the rest of us. I recently got in touch with Chris again after several years, and stopped at his house in 2004 to give him some copies of the wrestling show tapes. It was the first time he had seen any of it since back in the days when we did them. He was absolutely blown away to be able to see the footage again. It was nice to see Chris again after all those years.

Chris Hanson.

I recently came into contact with Mike Bauer (Rack-n-Roll Express) through email. Mike now lives in Missouri and has his hands full with three adopted boys. The kids are his life, and he is very happy with them. Mike was always good with kids as he spent a lot of time with the kids in our lightweight division back in the day. He is still good friends with his former tag team partner Chris Barger who works for a law firm out on the west coast.

Troy Steenerson (Slick Steenerson) still lives in Anoka, MN where he is married and has a small boy, Troy junior, who is now close to the age of 12. I stayed in touch with Troy for several years after the wrestling show. Back in 1998, I was honored when Troy asked me to be his best man at his wedding. Although we have not seen each other in nearly five years now, Troy still remains a good friend of mine. Troy and I had a lot of good times both on and off the wrestling show and there is always a story to talk about when looking back at our friendship.

Both John Hoffman (The Destructors) and his cousin Leslie Johnson (The Mystery Man) now work in the world of boxing. Where Leslie is boxing official, John is a semi-retired professional boxer and now one of the biggest boxing promoters in the state of Minnesota. I recently had a chance to visit his boxing gym up in Anoka, MN, and it was really great seeing John again. I have also been in touch with Leslie over the phone, and we all just love talking about the old wrestling days, no surprise there.

Leslie Johnson and John Hoffman.

Jamie McParland (The Irish Terror) is a teacher/instructor out on the west coast in the great state of Oregon. I recently got in touch with Jamie again and we talked for hours about the old days. In addition to teaching, Jamie also spends time playing the guitar and skateboarding. We are both looking forward to being able to meet each other again in the near future, if our schedules will ever work.

As for Charley Lane (Luxury Lane), we have always remained in touch with each other. After collage, Charley got married and now has four children and is doing very well in running his own business. Still living in northern Minnesota, Charley has become a developer and sets up and manages assisted living centers all over the state (and a few neighboring states). Although we had always stayed in touch by way of phone, we recently had the chance to meet each other again back in 2004 in Anoka. It was great to see each other after all these years. We had a great time. I told Charley how much I appreciated his friendship over all these years, and he likewise said the same thing to me. Friends like Charley are a rare thing, they are the kind that you can always count on, and that is why we have remained friends this long.

Charley Lane.

And finally, for myself, after graduating with an associates degree in 1990, I moved to Central Wisconsin and have lived in Schofield, WI ever since. I have managed to run three very successful businesses, two of which I still own. But for the past year now, I have been very busy with the entire NWF look back. From the DVDs to the book, it has taken a lot of my time. But it has been time well spent, and I enjoy each and every minute of it. Everyday I get emails from other kids and wrestling fans wanting to ask me questions about the NWF, and I answer each and every email I receive. I am truly lucky to have lived the life that I have with the wrestling show, and if I was ever given the chance to go back and do it all over again, I would do it in a heartbeat.

-Shawn "Crusher" Crossen

About The Author

Shawn Crossen.

For nearly 20 years, Shawn Crossen has waited to share his kids' wrestling league experiences with the rest of the world. When he was 14 years old, he started his very own kids pro wrestling league back in 1984. Within just two short years, he was producing a weekly cable tv show and holding live public events in front of hundreds of loyal fans. But going from his basement to a professionally sized wrestling ring was not an easy task, there were many obstacles along the way. Now, for the first time, he has come forth with a true story about his youthful dreams and accomplishments so incredible, you may find it hard to believe that it really actually happened.

For more information on the history of *NWF Kids Pro Wrestling*, please visit us on the web at: http://www.nwfwrestling.net

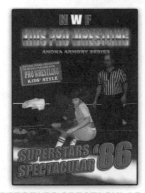